Unbro

My Life as a Truth Teller

By Kevin D. Annett

Remembering speechlessly, we seek the great forgotten language, the lost lane-end into heaven, a stone, a leaf, an unfound door.

– Thomas Wolfe, <u>You Can't Go Home Again</u>

What is to give light must endure burning.

– Victor Frankl, <u>Man's Search for Meaning</u>

Acknowledgement

For the ones who you don't see and can't imagine,

for the part of you free to give birth in the face of monsters,

and for the children.

Table of Contents

Prelude

One of my favourite words in Greek is *aletheia*, which means "truth that cannot be denied". The very idea is like a trumpet blast shattering glass, like when Thomas Jefferson and some of his friends overturned an Empire by holding certain things to be *self-evident*.

The idea of undeniability is a dangerous one for criminals and liars because there is no way they can wiggle away from what its accusing finger points to, like disinterred corpses. Even for the rest of us, undeniable truths are never comfortable ones because they threaten to upset the necessary lies that govern our lives. It's small wonder that *aletheia* has no English equivalent, considering our language's exquisite double-meaning capacity to obfuscate what is.

Over my considerable years and thanks to tackling some formidable Goliaths, I've been awarded and perhaps cursed with the label of a Truth Teller. In my case, the appellation has been bestowed because I've revealed and spoken of atrocities that people do not want to hear about, especially in

Canada. Sigmund Freud observed that what we call modern civilization survives only because "civilized" people do not normally speak what is true. That makes Truth Tellers a problem to any society because they speak honestly in and out of season, without regard to the requirements of civilization.

Like Christianity or Democracy, Truth Telling is a nice idea in theory but wholly disruptive in practice. I have had the fortune to survive the practice with a story to tell. May that tale unsettle you past the point of no return: especially nowadays.

Chapter One: Beginnings

Somebody messed up on the day I was born. Despite being big and noisy, I was placed among the maternity ward preemies. So, there I was: out of place and upsetting all the arrangements from the start.

My arrival was not so much a birth as a hijacking, thanks to being Caesarian sectioned into life. Even though my entering the world was involuntary, I've been imprudently assured by both my parents that of all three of their children, I was the only one who was wanted.

My ninety-one-year-old father Bill had another observation of my arrival, shared recently over bourbon.

"Even before you opened your eyes you kept pushing your arms out, over and over, like you were taking on the world."

Just four days after I first drew breath, a pudgy peasant in power named Lenny Khrushchev made the same bellicose gesture as me by officially knocking down a false god named Joseph Stalin.

I like to think that my arrival had something to do with his fall. Toppling murderous heads of state eventually became a habit of mine.

The day of my birth was a cold one, occurring in Edmonton in February. Barely five miles away, other newborns were paying the price for their brown skins at the Charles Camsell Indian Hospital. I never met the survivors of that extermination until more than forty years had passed, which tells you something.

I was almost born an American. After his obligatory stint as a grunt at Fort Dix, New Jersey, my Yankee father yielded to his own Dad's pressure to emigrate with his brood to the Great White North, with me in the womb. Perhaps that's why I've always felt misplaced in Canada and why I never apologize when I'm bumped into.

We didn't remain in Edmonton for long, especially after I stopped breathing regularly. My chronic bronchial asthma whisked us off to Toronto's Sick Children's Hospital where I learned to find meaning inside an oxygen tent at the age of two.

I can't say it was a completely dull experience. Quite a lot of fun stuff happened to me there, akin to what was being done to the Indian kids at the Camsell Hospital by some MKULTRA geeks. But at least it got us the hell out of Edmonton in winter.

My first recollections in life were not just of hospital wards but of Cabbage Town's usual attractions, like Old Fort York on the waterfront. My parents were obsessed with historical Canadian sites. By the age of four I could recite the tour guide's monologue about the pewter mugs on the kitchen sideboard of Governor Simcoe's house, or of the specifications of the brass cannons defying the perfidious Yanks lurking across Lake Ontario. My older brother Bill junior and I relived the War of 1812 incessantly, armed with our brocaded Fusilier uniforms and toy muskets complete with plastic bayonets that we levelled at the neighbours whenever we could.

Something from our Annett family past spoke out of that boyhood hankering to cry havoc and let slip the dogs of war. The first Annett to come to Canada, a Baptist farmer named Philip, arrived in 1820 from Wiltshire, England. He wasn't exactly a timid or retiring guy, for one day he took up arms against the colonial government in our aborted Canadian revolution of 1837. And yet his own Dad Robert had been a loyal British Army officer who'd commanded an infantry square in the thick of the slaughter fest known as the Battle of Waterloo and somehow survived. As a reward from a grateful Crown, Captain Robert was given the turf on which his son Phil would plot insurrection: two hundred acres of other peoples' land near what is now Watford, Ontario.

Rebels and loyalists, my family has been them all. From early on, it was clear to me what side of that great divide I had landed on.

Some time in my fifth year of life my folks decided to Go West, Young Fam, and the four of us left stuffy Tory Ontario for the great expanse beyond the Lakehead. Apparently, the dry prairie air was considered best for my lungs. Another attraction was that all my mother's McOuat family were camped in Winnipeg, along with six generations of ancestors who had come under duress from the Scottish Lowlands. Winnipeg became home for me.

Something happens when you leave the ancient geology of the Canadian Shield and spill out onto the flat land. The air feels palpably free and infused with a brooding mystery. That part of the nation has always been a magnet for dreamers and wanderers. It found in me a kindred soul and nurtured a resonance of which I was barely conscious even as it grew over time.

Two Metis rebellions, a General Strike and many smaller battles for justice had erupted in Winnipeg before we Annetts arrived there in the summer of 1961. Some of those fights between Haves and Have Nots had touched our wider family. My mother Margaret's family had relatives on both sides of the Riel Rebellion. As a young man, her father Walter McOuat had been just a few paces from one of the men shot to death by Mounties rampaging down Portage street on Bloody Sunday during the 1919 General Strike. As good hearted as they were, my mom's relatives were raised in a perpetual climate of fear about their French and aboriginal neighbours: one of the legacies of these upheavals. My mother used to routinely issue me stern warnings to stay out of Winnipeg's North End, "full of Indians, Communists and Jews".

Naturally, I ignored her.

The Met movie house on Donald street sat on the edge of the North End. On Saturday afternoons, assorted cousins along with throngs of other young boys joined me in making purposeful mayhem in its balcony as forgettable action flics strove fruitlessly to command our attention. Helping us lob popcorn bags and drinks onto unsuspecting viewers were the Indian and Metis kids from across the invisible divide. Our ranks normally didn't mix, since the theatre was segregated, but when they did blood was spilled, mostly from busted noses. The brown skins usually won our fights because they were ruthless, and they really wanted us dead.

After one of these punch-ups where I'd fared the worst, my Dad encountered me in our bathroom applying a wet cloth to my bruises. He gazed at me solemnly from behind a wreath of cigarette smoke and remarked,

"Pretty ironic, isn't it? You being related to them"

That's when I discovered we had Injuns in the family.

Her name was Sarah Jourdain and she was a full blood Cree from Stoney Mountain. She lingers subversively in my Mother's family tree like a latter-day Pope Joan, scrubbed from the history books but not totally from our memory. One of my great grandfather's brothers had married her in a very un-Presbyterian moment and they had had a kid together. But that's where the hushed narrative ends. None of my mom's McOuat clan ever talked about Sarah.

My great-grandfather in question was David Duncan McOuat. He was an irascible old bastard who busted up the illicit crossbreeding romance by his brother and That Heathen Woman. As a young man, "D.D." had led vigilante raids to hunt down and kill the Metis rebel Louis Riel. When he was older, and as one of the richest men in Winnipeg, D.D. earned the applause of a Free Press editorial after he personally flogged a stranger with his whip for tying his horse to D.D.'s gold plated hitching post outside his lumber business. In the same magisterial vein, he disowned his eldest son, my grandfather Walter, for marrying an Irish girl, my grandma Grace.

Clearly, D.D. knew a thing or two about preserving Civilization as he knew it.

Of course, Canadians normally don't have to be subjected to such harsh methods; they generally know how to behave and what to believe without requiring the whip. As I grew up in Winnipeg, the unseen divides stayed intact, and we usually kept to our own. One exception was in 1968 when my parents tried taking John Hirsh to lunch with them at the prestigious Carleton Club. John headed the Manitoba Theatre Centre, but he was also a Jew and an Auschwitz survivor. So, the Carleton staff followed the Rules and showed him the door. My folks quit the Club in disgust, but the No Jews policy remained.

Of course, by that time I had my own battles to contend with at the private boys' school where my parents had deposited me like a credulous David Copperfield. St. Johns Ravenscourt was Winnipeg's version of Eton and Harrow: a breeding ground for the sons of Prime Ministers and corporate tycoons. The school had been around for a century, as had some of its teachers. One of them was a seriously deranged Yorkshireman named Harry Shepherd who habitually grabbed pupils by the hair on their temples and twisted violently, sometimes raising the screaming boy right out of his seat. Harry's eyes would dance with pleasure at his handiwork. Straps, canes, and knuckles routinely fell on our soft and unprotected parts.

I didn't make things any easier by asking questions that my teachers no doubt considered impertinent. One instance among many stands out, from Grade Five. Our social studies teacher, Mrs. Watson, was exclaiming to us over a map of the world how much of it lay within the "civilizing" influence of the British Empire. As she made her point by swinging her yard stick to all the red-colored countries, I put up my hand, genuinely wanting to know the truth as I asked her,

"If the Empire is so great, how come there are so many starving people in it?".

Neither the blows to my hands issued by Mrs. Watson and her yardstick nor my occupancy of a chair in the hall for the rest of the day made any sense to me. All I knew is that she wouldn't answer my question.

My Dad couldn't afford to keep me ensconced at Ravenscourt for more than three years, but it seemed like thirty. I remember often having diarrhea or vomiting spells every morning before school, knowing what awaited me from not only psychotic teachers but my fellow students, who acted out the same violence on each other. My parents didn't catch on; or if they did, they never said anything.

A lot of other boys my age must have gone through a similar torture, because everybody in our 'hood was passing on the violence downwards. Captured prairie dogs, pet hamsters and any kid smaller than us received our bloody ministrations. My slaughter of choice was incinerating hundreds of ants at a time with lighter fluid and matches. Any of us who didn't own an air gun and use it against anything that moved was considered a loser. Rifle practice on stray cats and dogs was all in a day's fun.

My complicity in this carnage began to change for me when I was twelve, after something happened to me on the Ravenscourt school bus. One of our resident thugs named Brian Smith took a serious disliking to a diminutive Grade Three kid. But instead of whacking the boy himself he expected me to do it for him.

"Noogy him, Annett, or I'll noogy you!" he ordered as he grabbed me by the neck. I was too shocked to obey, so he tightened his grip and repeated the command.

For those of you who don't know the expression, a "noogy" consists of driving one's tightened knuckle into the cranium of a preferred victim with as much force as possible. The aim is to evoke maximum suffering on the target and maximum pleasure on the perpetrator.

I remember hovering in horror as the little kid turned to stare at me pitiably. I hesitated for a moment, until pain coursed through my head as Brian's formidable Noogy fell on me.

"Do it!" he shrieked. And I did so, automatically.

"Harder!" he commanded, and I complied. But the second time I hit the young boy he began to blubber and sob. His eyes fell on me with a look That I have never forgotten. And that stopped me.

"You fucking pansy, you keep noogying him!" Brian yelled at me, and he struck me even harder. But my hands had fallen to my side. I let the bully's blows rain down on me. With each new assault, I became even more determined not to hit the young boy anymore. Striking him was worse than being hit myself.

People are not born with compassion, or even with a soul. They need to be nurtured and grow in us. After the incident on the bus, something expanded in me. I stopped killing because suddenly I hated it. My own still, small voice of conscience had finally appeared.

Of course, my born-again pacifism at age twelve didn't garner me sudden treasures in heaven or on earth. On the contrary. Soon after my conversion, my beloved grandmother Grace McOuat was killed by God one night before we could say goodbye. Grandma had been at the centre of my heart and my extended family in Winnipeg, and now the heartbeat was gone.

My snug world collapsed after that. Jobless and nearly penniless, with creditors and cops snapping at his heels, my father suddenly announced we were moving to Vancouver. I didn't even know where that was. My mother Marg, ever sensitive to any chance to blame Dad for our misfortunes, went along with his scheme. Maybe they had gone nuts in a grief-crazed response to Grandma's death.

Regardless, soon after we planted Grace McOuat in St. Vital Cemetery alongside her beloved Walter, my folks, Bill junior, my wee sister Deirdre and yours truly packed ourselves off to the west coast. In an instant I was torn from all I knew and loved. It felt to me like I had died.

....

Another orphan had also passed my way, through the dark mountains that had claimed his life. Like my Annett ancestors, he came to Canada on a "coffin ship" loaded with hunger and death. But unlike the rest of his dispossessed Irish family, he survived the voyage. He had married, learned a trade as a railroad mechanic and settled with his Basque wife and six children in Revelstoke, British Columbia. His eldest child was my grandmother Grace. His name was Daniel Edward O'Neill and he died in the early hours of January 26, 1912 when a snow slide snuffed him out.

I didn't know the story about my Irish great-grandfather when my family and I journeyed through the pass where he'd died, as we relocated to Vancouver. For years, the truth of how Daniel died had remained as unmarked as the grave that held his body. One day I honored that site and his story by erecting a headstone that declared,

"Greater Love has no man than to give his life for others."

On the blizzardly night that he died, Grandpa Dan was called out on a rescue mission to Rogers Pass after the main Canadian Pacific Railway line had been cut by a snow slide. Dan and his work crew dug out a passenger car and helped the rescued people to safety, including a CPR official named James Fitzpatrick. Rather than return to Revelstoke with them, Dan stayed at his post and kept digging out another buried car. That's when a second slide hit and carried the car and Dan down into a river valley. They dug out his corpse two days later.

The next week, the man he'd rescued, his fellow Irishman James Fitzpatrick, informed Dan's widow Rose that she wasn't eligible for the paltry pension owed to her husband. That cruelty killed the family.

Impoverished and struggling, within two years Rose was dead and all the children were farmed out to relatives in Montreal.

When I was a man, Daniel O'Neill came to me in a dream. His words and presence were as lucid as the suffering aboriginal people I was meeting every day. Daniel said to me, "It's our story too, Kevin. We're all survivors of genocide."

Something of that encounter was foreshadowed when I first sensed my great-grandfather in Rogers Pass in the late summer of 1968. My own grief of being exiled from what I loved was like an echo of that pathos from Dan's life and our family past. I came to Vancouver as a boy who was immersed in a funeral shroud. But as we approached the coast, the mountains' mist parted, and we entered a resplendent valley and a sun-bathed sea. Like my own longing heart, the night gave way to an unexpected dawn.

Discovering girls had something to do with it.

That autumn, the opposite sex burst upon me like a wondrously unannounced kiss. Cloistered in a boys' school since I was eight years old, I was more than slightly overwhelmed by the torrent of female attention that welcomed me to University Hill Secondary School. I was the cute new boy in the neighbourhood, unaware of my own easy and natural charm.

Thus equipped, I began to get asked out by a welter of young women and learned firsthand what all the songs were about. On one memorable day, a giggling crowd of a dozen grade seven girls followed me home after school and, catching up with me (I didn't run that fast), held me down and spread delighted kisses on me for a considerable amount of time.

And thus did something other than sadness mark my first months in high school, as I learned to accept affection and self-esteem. I even started to enjoy schooling and came to love the forested peace of our new home on the University of BC campus. My father had found a brief sinecure in his cousin Jim's stock broking firm, and once again he could pay the rent and pass muster with Mommy Dearest. Things were looking up at Planet Annett.

But then the Indians arrived.

Our newfound bourgeois credentials as a materially "respectable" family had earned us a place in the local United Church pews, even though I annoyed our nebbish of a clergyman during my confirmation class by asking him questions about the Bible that he couldn't answer.

As was her wont, my mother soon became Sunday School Superintendent. As such, she came up with the rather odd idea to hold an exchange visit with a northern aboriginal community in Hazelton, B.C. Imagine! A gang of barely clad and tuberculosis - ridden Indian kids barrelling around the lily-white environs of University Hill; and a similar number of Pale Johnnies and Susies camping out in a slummy, lice-filled reservation hundreds of miles from the nearest jacuzzi!

I still don't know whether Mom was simply naïve or suicidal. I also don't recall how she pulled it off, besides her relying on the congenital need for white liberals in Canada to prove that they're not racists. The novel exchange visit went ahead, even though it spelled eventual doom for our Annett family in that neighbourhood and church. But before the big boot fell, my life was blown wide open by the experience.

Our church group travelled from University Hill to Hazelton as the first leg of the exchange. It was like entering another world, which of course it was.

The strangers were called Tsimshians, but the word meant nothing to me. In a valley surrounded by towering mountains at the junction of two rivers, a village of two hundred people greeted us. I had never encountered such poverty and desolation.

Many of the local children were gone from the village, grabbed and trucked far away to Edmonton where they were incarcerated and incinerated at a thing called an "Indian residential school". Of the kids who remained, Rosie Shanoss stands out in my memory. She was my introduction to the Canadian Holocaust.

The jagged scar that ran across her little forehead wasn't the worst of it. Nor was the sickly yellow ooze that dripped from her nose, or her perpetual cough, or the rickets that bent her legs. It was the look in her eyes that horrified me: a pure animal terror. Those eyes told the story that no-one wants to hear.

Hazelton had the historical advantage of occupying a *cul de sac* situated off the main road from the germ warfare and mass murder that swept across the west coast after gold was discovered in the 1850's. The black robes had come late to this land but no less murderously.

Our group's host, an older United Church minister named Gordon Faris, pretended to know the local Indians even as they avoided him like the plague he embodied. The only other churchman in the area was an Oblate priest in the nearby village of Kispiox, whose Indians were ordered by the cleric not to mingle with their "pagan" relatives in Hazelton. Despite this relatively minimal church presence, the usual devastating signs of prolonged contact with the "Mu-multh-nees", or "ghost people", as the Tsimshians called us, were everywhere to be seen.

I couldn't get Rosie's eyes out of my mind on the first night after our arrival. I was too frightened to talk about it with anyone. But my father, who had come along on the trip as an adult supervisor, noticed my mood. Unable to sleep, I had wandered upstairs from Gordon Faris' basement where all of the boys were sprawled in our sleeping bags. Dad was standing by the kitchen sink.

"Had a bad dream?" he said, puffing his inevitable cigarette.

"What's wrong with these people, Dad?" I asked.

"That's a long story" he muttered.

"What about that girl with the big cut on her head?"

Dad shrugged, extinguishing the butt in the sink.

"Her father did it to her when he was drunk. Did a lot worse to her, too. At least that's what the Reverend says."

I was trying to figure out what he meant by that when Dad said gravely,

"Kev, there used to be thousands of those people here. Most of them got wiped out by us. You never forget that."

His words put everything in a different light. I knew Dad was right, just by looking around the village.

After my time in Hazelton, killing Indians was no longer something I did in my imagination as I shot my toy rifle at the "redskins" lurking behind wheat bales on our family journeys across the prairie each summer. Suddenly it wasn't a game. The brown children who stared at me like I was their personal enemy were survivors of something horrible and beyond belief. And it all scared the crap out of me.

Still, none of it was as real as my own life at the time. My adolescent mind tucked away the dawning truth, even after our group departed Hazelton with a clutch of Indian kids in tow, bound for our plush University Hill neighbourhood. The aboriginals were the strangers now, on our turf and at our behest. And like any unpleasant reminder, the Indians were expected to behave themselves. And my mother was expected to make sure they behaved.

Mom never liked to be told what to do – I come by the trait honestly – especially when so instructed by the big moneyed Tartuffians who ran our local church. The latter put Ma on notice that if anything went untoward during the savages' week in their neighbourhood, she'd be held responsible. And they demanded that all the native kids be x-rayed and screened for tuberculosis before they set one foot on their Holy of Holies. Mom told them she wouldn't insult the Indians like that. Her impudence was noted.

The Pharisees need not have worried. The last group of folks to cause mayhem are traumatized, impoverished Indian children facing the loaded gun called Canada. Besides, it wasn't their behaviour that was the problem; their presence in our neighbourhood was.

For the first time in my life, I encountered the hate stare from otherwise placid pale Canadians: like when I first walked with our billeted Indian, a kid named Arnold, to the local drugstore for a treat. Like an early version of COVID-hysterics, everyone gave us a wide berth, gaping at me like I was insane or infected with a plague. On the way home the Mounties stopped the two of us. The cops threw Arnold in the back of their cruiser and grilled me for an hour. They couldn't believe the Indian was with me.

A similar retribution fell on my family soon after the dark strangers had departed.

Within a week, my mother was expelled as Sunday School Superintendent and we found ourselves unwelcome at University Hill United Church. Then my family was forced out of the neighbourhood after my father was visited and threatened with dire consequences by two local church and university big shots, Dr. Charles Kerr and William Sauder.

Both of those men now have UBC campus buildings named after them, by the way.

Well, Holy Foreshadowing, Batman! Perhaps it was only fitting that a quarter century later I would do a repeat performance and undergo a similar fate by the same church for also allowing room in the pews for those feared Others. The Pharisees are nothing if not consistent. But at the time, all I felt was a disgusted loathing for the cruelty and hypocrisy of the Sunday Christians.

The experience made me a determined atheist at the ripe old age of fifteen, as once again my world fell apart.

....

I never let my schooling interfere with my education.
– Mark Twain

The place was once a forest so thick that sunlight didn't reach the soil. By the time I lived there the soil and the towering cedar trees were gone, replaced by concrete. Winos and addicts slept in the apartment hallway of what passed briefly as our home. The clatter of Vancouver's West End never ceased, so we always kept our windows shut. But at least the busses ran on time. It took more than an hour for them to get me and my siblings to school, where my pampered University Hill friends looked at me askance when I tried explaining to them where I lived now.

In our teens we tend to be as supple emotionally as we are physically. I was, at least. I learned to flow around our domestic family strife – not just the poverty and uncertainty but my parents' constant squabbling – and find my own happiness. But the experience left me as little inclined towards family life as I was towards religion after the University Hill United Church debacle. I increasingly went my own way.

By the time I was sixteen, my own way meant radical politics, and what is today tritely called "left-wing activism". I became a convinced Marxist.

I like to thank Limpy Lower for launching me down that revolutionary road. Limpy was our school's Vice Principal and a born asshole. He held sway as the "adult supervisor" on our high school student council, the not exactly august body to which I was elected in grade nine because I was cute and popular.

Old Limpy – who had acquired his nickname and disability from a German bullet during the Battle of the Somme – took an instant disliking to me during our brief time together on the council, especially when I strayed from acceptable topics like fund raising for school dances. I wanted a Drop In for the students, but Limpy said no. I suggested we hold open student assemblies where anyone could speak and vote, but Limpy vetoed my affrontery as deftly as he used to pick off Krauts. And so on.

Well, I'd finally had enough. One memorable lunch hour I put forward a motion in the student council to dispense with our adult supervisor, The Big Limp himself. The room went silent. Nobody dared to speak, except Mr. Lower himself, who shot at me like I was an advancing Hun,

"What did you say?"

"It's called self-government" I replied sarcastically. "You know, democracy. It's a Greek idea. Ever heard of it?".

I was ordered to leave the room and never return.

It was with a deep-seated delight that I spent that same evening composing an incendiary tract on the free typewriter in the basement of the Sedgewick Library on campus. The next morning with the help of a friend my leaflet appeared in fifty copies in the hallways of our school, its message spreading like a deadly virus through my staid Alma Mater:

"How can we be citizens of a democracy as adults when we're not allowed to practice democracy as students? We don't need an adult to supervise us like we're good little boys and girls. We need a free and independent student council. Until we get one, we should Boycott Student Council Elections and Not Pay our Student Council Fees! Mr. Lower has to go!"

I didn't sign my fiery manifesto, but everyone knew who had written it: including Limpy Lower. He tried nabbing me in the hall the next day, but I easily outran the old fart and hid in the nearby woods. By then, the school was in an uproar. I'd become an overnight pariah. Teachers gave me hate stares and students flashed excited but wary looks.

Soon after, the Principal personally escorted me out of the school building and told me forebodingly that "higher authorities" would soon be in touch with my parents about my behaviour.

The upshot of it all was my first hard lesson in realpolitik: *Don't rely on anyone to act for you, or to do what they promise.* My erstwhile friends who swore to stand by me when the boot came down suddenly vanished, especially the following week when I was hauled before the Superintendent of the Vancouver School Board. I figured he was about to keel-haul me prior to my permanent expulsion from school. Instead, the guy offered me a seat on a new provincial government commission to reform education.

Lesson Two: *If your adversaries can't crush you, they'll try buying you.*

And, of course, Lesson Three: *Don't be bought.*
Just remain a threat.

When the smoke cleared for me, I was elated to
learn that unlike what I had been taught, I could
have a real impact on an unjust and apparently
immovable world. As the book of high school closed
for me, an even bigger one opened.

My real education had begun. I knew myself to be
a permanent revolutionary.

Chapter Two: Youth and Rebellion

We don't want money. We don't want power. We want a new world.
– Graffiti in a Santiago slum, 1972

Either you want in or you want out. You make your choice and the rest follows.
– Joe Hendsbee to the author, 1974

Even before Carlos spoke to me, all that mattered was in his eyes.

We'd met at a union picnic when I was nineteen. His children startled me that day by diving in panic under a table when a helicopter sounded in the distance.

"They haven't got over it" he explained.

It had been touch and go for all of them after the Chilean coup. Carlos was head of his Workers' Co-operative and a prominent Socialist Party leader, which made him doubly targeted by the military. They caught him one day and tortured him badly in a prison near the Valparaiso docks. But his worst pain was not knowing where his children were, after his wife was shot. Eventually he was reunited with his children and they escaped to Mexico.

"I knew the mother of one of my guards and he got me out one night, or I'd have been dead" Carlos told me.

"They weren't all gorillas. Many of the soldiers would have come over to us. We could have won our revolution. That's why we can't ever give up."

When I was very young, I often took bread out of the baker's truck and shared it freely with my friends. Despite my mother's admonitions, the concept of money was lost on me, like the strange idea that people should go hungry just because they lacked cash. The same spirit caused me to routinely give away our family's belongings to those around us who needed them more.

"You see?" I said excitedly to my Mom one Sunday after church as I quoted from the Bible's Book of Acts.

"It says that none of the first Christians owned anything. They shared it all out of love, so there was nobody rich and nobody poor."

Carlos Ortega and his people had the same dream. Like the founder of that great banquet of loving equality, they were crucified for trying to make it a living force in the world. As I came to know those exiled revolutionaries, a whisper of their spirit went from their heart to my own. Even as their dream drifted and faded above the bombed factories and slums across their homeland, it found fertile soil in other lives that would carry on mankind's oldest hope. It found such good ground in me.

My life's course was set during that time. The idea of living only for myself, of following a career path and piling up loot and security, was as repugnant to me as mugging an old lady for her wallet. I knew in my guts that I could only find meaning in something more than myself, in the cause of a humanity struggling to free itself of violence and exploitation, and of all the crushing weights and divisions.

The harmony that other men find in an easy chair or an easier job I discovered by engaging in the everyday lives and battles of people around me. I hated what was wrong and unjust. Whatever caused someone to get screwed over for another felt like an assault on me personally. I could not stand by unmoved and watch people be destroyed. I only wanted to do what was true and good and live my life without compromise, unsoiled by the complicity in society's violent corruption that is expected of all of us. I couldn't imagine a home except in a future, just world. That spirit made me a mystery and eventually a peril in the minds of my family and friends.

During those years, I met and took to my heart a hardened old longshoreman named Joe Hendsbee. We'd met at Spartacus Books, the radical hangout in downtown Vancouver where I worked as a volunteer. Joe had seen and been it all.

A blacklisted Communist and union dissident, a veteran of a hundred unwinnable battles including the Spanish Civil War, Joe had been shot, stabbed, beaten to a pulp and thrown in jail more times than he could recall. But he wore none of his sixty-seven years as weariness or regret. He accepted all the sorrows of his life as a triumph, as the inevitable consequence of being who he was: an unrepentant revolutionary.

One night after he'd shocked the Spartacus Books crowd by suggesting that instead of worrying and bitching about the rent increase they should go out and shoot the landlord, Joe invited me to the Lotus Hotel for a few brewskies.

We went alone. Our politically correct associates at the bookstore never frequented the Lotus pub after the place introduced female strippers, but Joe and I loved the crowd. They were mostly waterfront and city workers, and displaced Indians with too much to tell, like Ronnie Jack the Retard. For a couple of bucks, Ronnie would recite his poems about his abduction and seduction by nubile female aliens who turned out to be working for the feds.

On that particular night, Ronnie was nowhere in sight, and the pub's usual clientele was sparse. The unusual quiet fit my somber mood. Joe picked up on it and tried to lighten things with a bad joke, but I wasn't biting.

"So, what's eatin' you?" he asked me between swigs from his Molson.

I couldn't frame my feelings, and instead picked at my beer bottle's label.

"I had a guy like you on my swabbin' crew once" Hendsbee remarked.

"Goddamn it, he was a sober son of a bitch. Always gripin' 'bout sumpthin'. One day he blew his brains out."

"That's great" I muttered morosely. I stared at him and asked,

"How do you deal with all the bullshit in the world?"

The man chortled.

"Bourbon. Getting' laid. The occasional line of cocaine."

"That's all crap and you know it" I barked at him. "I'm serious, man"

Hendsbee finished his beer and regarded me thoughtfully.

"I never let their shit get to me, is all" he answered.

"But Christ, Joe, how can it not? You've had two failed marriages, you're blacklisted and broke, you've got no friends or family I can see ..."

"I got you" he observed, lighting up a stogie.

"And I still got my balls."

"You know what I mean! You're fighting the same fights as fifty years ago and you're near seventy."

He shook his head like I was Ronnie.

"Yeah? So what? I'm a goddamned radical! It comes with the territory"

"But if you had to do it again ..." I began, but he cut in.

"Wouldn't change a fuckin' thing. Either you got principles, or you don't. If you got 'em, you do 'em."

He could see I was still dissatisfied.

"It's like when they offered me a management spot if I left the union and I told 'em to shove it up their ass. Either you want in or you want out. You make your choice and the rest follows."

I had already made my own choice by then, and we both knew it. I wanted out, and badly, from an insane society. But so much else had to follow from my yearning for freedom.

....

I left Vancouver in the new year of 1976, bound for the steel mills of Hamilton, Ontario. Like my buddy Joe Hendsbee, I had signed on full-time for the revolution when I was barely twenty.

We called ourselves the International Socialists (IS). Born from a left-wing split out of the New Democratic Party, the group was mostly college students without much life experience who fancied themselves equipped to lead ten million Canadian workers to the socialist promised land.

The sheer balsyness of such infantile hubris impressed me and won me as an early IS recruit. What mattered to me more than knowledge or political savvy was the determination and the will to overcome any obstacle. I was in a visceral and permanent revolt against society. I sought only the most radical action to overturn the entire sick mess. Revolutionary socialism fit the bill.

Still, I felt out of place in the IS from the start, since I'd never read Das Kapital and couldn't match the smooth phrase mongering and inbred clique culture of the group, personified in the three graduate students from York University who'd proclaimed themselves as our IS "leadership".

I could see that to these three, who set the tone for the group, revolution was a nice idea that had less to do with human beings than with their own academic careers.

Our group of thirty "Toy Bolsheviks" was scattered precariously across southern Ontario, in Toronto, Ottawa and Hamilton. In our transplanted Leninist worldview, the industrial working class constituted the strategic force for revolution in Canada. But only a few of us were willing to colonize ourselves among blue collar proletarians. I was one of those few, naturally. And so, like the proverbial sacrificial lamb, I hurried to Hamilton during a frigid January to seek employment in its steel mills.

In truth, my move was also prompted by my aversion to the flaccid talk-shop atmosphere of the Toronto-centered IS. I wanted to change the world by building a revolutionary party of action on the ground, not by debating the matter. Just like years later in the United Church, I believed in all the nice words and tried putting them into practice, which is never a healthy undertaking in the company of lesser beings.

One of the more solid and decent IS comrades was an autoworker named Mark Brett. He and his wife Kathy Denomy took a liking to me right away and gave me a couch to sleep on until I could find my own digs. But they made the mistake of giving me my first exposure of Hamilton's north end the night we drove into town, as the blast furnaces spilled their molten slag into the harbour and produced billowing mountains of steam. The scene resembled something out of Dante's Inferno.

"What the fuck ..." I mumbled from the back seat of their car.

"Still want to work in there?" Mark chuckled.

"Oh, shut up" his wife snapped at him, as she turned to give me a warm and sympathetic gaze. Kathy always did it for me.

Finding work wasn't a problem. The steel mills weren't hiring, but a rail car manufacturer was.

"Got any trade experience?" the job interviewer asked me.

"Well, I've sorted mail ..."

"You done mechanical fitting? Welding assist?"

"Uh, no …" I mumbled, my hopes sinking.

"Fuck it. I'll stick you on No. 3 crew, they got a vacancy for a fitter. You can learn on the job" he declared, handing me a form and gesturing towards the deafening and cavernous assembly plant of National Steel Car.

Working there wasn't so bad, if you didn't mind losing your hearing and gagging every minute on welding fumes. That first day on the line was as akin to warfare as I could have imagined, like the torrent of screaming metal that my grandfather Ross Annett endured when at the same age as me he slogged through the killing fields of Flanders. Even wearing my safety glasses, I had to routinely swab out of my eyes the pieces of steel embedded there by the metal grinder I operated. I could barely see through my swollen lids by the end of the shift. The veterans on my welding crew thought it was all quite funny.

"Consider yourself lucky, dip shit" one of the welders remarked to me.

"Last month a fitter lost his nuts when his grinder came apart."

In my nearly blind condition after my first shift, I spent an hour hobbling to Kathy and Mark's place. They were already in bed, but Kathy was on me like a mother hen.

"It's so stupid" she said as she dabbed at my eyes with a wet cloth. Her hand felt soft and soothing on my face, and I quickly forgot about my pain.

"At least I got a job, I'll be in the union soon" I answered, hoping she would touch me more.

"I don't care, Kevin. It's not worth it" she spouted angrily.

"Do you think McNally or Bakan would ever work in that hell hole? But they expect you to!"

Her reference to two of our "official" IS leaders made me chuckle, but then I jerked in pain when she touched a sore spot on my face.

"I'm sorry" she whispered, and unselfconsciously kissed the spot. Everything was fine after that.

After my first paycheque I found a place of my own: a north end fleabag apartment perched regretfully above a metal parts recycling depot. Thus situated, I was awakened every morning by the sound of barrels smashing together, as if to remind me that in Steel City, there was no escaping the cacophony of metal on metal.

To cheapen the rent, I shared my dingy abode with another IS comrade, an unemployed guy on social assistance named Barry Diacon. Barry had a severe depression problem and normally stayed holed up in his bedroom except when we held our weekly IS branch meeting. When I wasn't working a shift at Steel Car, I tried to entice Barry out to the local Sherman Pub for a few evening beers, but he never bit. Only when he joined me in flogging our group's newspaper *Workers' Action* at the morning shifts along factory row would Barry budge from his despondency. He was a man in a lot of unspoken pain that was unalleviated even by his living for the greater cause.

Life for me at twenty was simple, purposeful and obvious. I was living for the greatest reason one can live, and that was to raise up my fellow man by bringing down what kept him down. Devoted thus, I was deeply happy. But my consecration allowed no room for the limitations of others. My fidelity positioned me out in front of the crowd, and then as now, it left me there alone, since there were few who could match and share my Tip of the Spear commitment. That solitude led to a loneliness that wore at me and threatened to betray me.

I was still a virgin then, in every respect. After my brief high-school plunge into life around girls, I had pulled back from relationships. I became sad and serious. Our family's expulsion from University Hill and my parents' increasing slide into poverty had sobered me and made me acutely sensitive to the pain and injustice of the world. And it also filled me with a personal sense of responsibility to fight it.

Unfortunately or not, such zeal didn't allow much room for the happy and spontaneous part of me, or for a woman's love in my life. The more self-reliant I became, the safer and stronger I felt. The tender vulnerability of the heart had no place in my solid inner equation.

Some people saw through my rough exterior. Kathy Denomy was one of them. On a memorable day soon after I landed in Hamilton, I arrived with uncharacteristic tardiness at a protest rally.

Kathy and Mark were waiting for me at the event with a wad of leaflets to distribute to passersby. With a wink and a wry grin, Mark said,

"Hey Kev! We thought you weren't going to make it. What happened, did you finally get laid?"

Before I could answer, Kathy lit into him angrily.

"Don't be stupid, Mark! Kevin's too beautiful for any of that!"

I began to fall in love with her even more after that day. Whenever I imagined what domestic bliss would be like, Kathy Denomy's shining face came to mind. It was a new experience for me to be seen and understood by a woman, and to be so loved and admired. It became easier for me to smile on some days.

Meanwhile, our Sisyphean political task remained. In a town of 300,000 souls, a mere handful of us were committed to acting as one to create a new society. The dilemma faced us every moment: how do people endure as revolutionaries amid the old, corrupting regime? How do we encourage and rally others to fight for small gains without losing sight of the bigger purpose, of overthrowing all that oppresses them? How do we make people want to risk and struggle when they don't even believe in themselves? Is the vision ever enough by itself?

My spirit was willing, but the flesh faltered. After seven weeks in National Steel Car my asthmatic lungs threatened to permanently pack it in from all the welding fumes. My constant wheezing alarmed Kathy to no end. She insisted that I quit my job.

"I'll be alright" I insisted.

"You'll be fucking dead, Kev"

I chuckled at her unusual profanity. But she didn't laugh. Her eyes filled with tears.

Kathy needn't have worried. The next week I was fired by a foreman who had it in for me after I spouted off to my fellow proles about our crappy working conditions.

Like a lot of other guys in town, I was suddenly on the scrap heap. But unlike them, and much to the chagrin of my IS "party bosses" in Toronto, I didn't scurry off to find another crappy job. Instead, with my surplus of free time, I started writing my first novel.

The plot was predictably autobiographical. Its protagonist is a young unemployed Communist named Samuel Wedge who struggles in southern Saskatchewan during the worst of the Depression years.

Torn between helping his farming family and seeking a job in Regina, Sam throws himself into full-time party work as an agitator in a local "Relief Camp" of jobless men near Weyburn. After being beaten senseless by cops and landing in jail, Sam is mended and romanced by a married comrade named Marcy, whose resemblance to the real-life Kathy Denomy is more than passing. Marcy wants to leave her husband for Sam, but she never finds the nerve to do it. Sam's heart, in turn, becomes as broken as the prairie soil, and he throws himself with suicidal fervour into even greater danger.

At that point in my opus I ran out of juice, or more honestly, writing it became caustic, as art began reflecting life too closely. I hadn't realized how existentially lonely I was, and how nothing in my chosen life could help me navigate my inner scars. My days were devoted to our cause, and my nights were consumed in a pain I did not understand. My life, like my novel, hung in abeyance.

I've never been one to stare blankly at a wall for long. The darker became my mood, the stronger was my will to do something. After a month of being out of work, I suggested to my IS comrades that we hold a rally for the thousands of local unemployed people and start organizing them to get better benefits. The pittance of $212 a month I received on assistance did not even cover my rent.

One of our IS branch members named Stuart, the only college student among us, looked down his nose at the idea, pronouncing,

"The unemployed don't make revolutions. Just read Marx."

My retort was plain enough.

"Who's talking revolution? I'm talking fucking survival!"

As I've often observed, there's a fundamental difference between acting from a good intention and doing so because your life depends on it.

The other IS comrades went for my idea. We began leafletting local pubs and Unemployment Insurance offices, gathering recruits. The next week we called a protest at City Hall and over fifty people showed up. Out of that we formed the Hamilton Union of the Unemployed and I was elected its Secretary.

Our new group started raising hell all over the city. We occupied the Mayor's office and were called commies and bums by His "Lardship", a real estate shark named John A. MacDonald (seriously). Then we started blockading the doors of the UI offices and were arrested, but we made the headlines in the process with our catchy slogans like "*Robin Hood was Right!*". We even got some of the local unions to fund us and give me a platform to speak at their meetings about our cause: not just the fight to win a living wage but to overturn the crazy capitalist system responsible for our misery.

"You like to run for public office?" a Steelworkers' Union official asked me after a fiery talk I'd given to his local.

"What, you mean for the NDP?" I said.

"Fuck yeah, who do you think? I'll nominate your ass. You're a smart kid and we can use you."

And that point I whipped out a copy of my IS party newspaper *Workers' Action* and flashed it in his face with a grin. The union bureaucrat gave our radical rag a single, horrified look and clammed up. I was never invited back.

My first wife Judy, who I met at a rally shortly after this incident, told me some years later that I'd have gotten a lot further in life without all my principles mucking up the works. Maybe so. But hell, everybody's got principles; it's what you do with them that decides whether you're in or out, to paraphrase Joe Hendsbee.

An old guy a lot like Joe crossed my path at that time. His name was Don Eperson. I met him one evening on my way home from a meeting. He was holding a solitary vigil outside the Royal Bank, carrying a placard that read *"Feed the Poor, Starve the Bankers!"*.

"What the hell do you want?" Don barked at me when I stopped to gape at his sign.

"The place is locked up" I pointed out with a gesture at the dark building.

"So, who gives a fuck, smartass? You think them thieving bastards ever sleep?"

Don and I took to each other right away. He was seventy-eight years old and a veteran of all the unemployed battles of the Dirty Thirties. He'd had bullets and firehoses drilled at him, and seen his best friend shot through the heart by a Montreal cop during a food riot.

Don Eperson was part of our living but suppressed history: the kind that's never taught in schools. He was stuffed to the gills with a hard-earned wisdom about the way the world really operated. I helped him share that savvy with many others when I gave him a platform at our unemployed rallies.

Don loved to blast his beleaguered audiences, and he always did so to their applause:

"I been getting it up the ass my whole life by this fucked up system! I been out of work for a quarter of my life! But I got hope and I'll tell you why! It's 'cause for every one of them rich greedy bastards who run this country there's a million of us! We could wipe 'em out tomorrow and take back this country! That's up to every single one of you here to make happen! So, quit your bitchin', get the fuck off your ass and join up with us now before it's your life that's ripped to pieces!"

Judy Wright was in the crowd that cheered Don on the evening of May 9, 1978. The old guy was elated but exhausted after the meeting. I had just fetched him some coffee when a young blonde-haired woman I couldn't help but notice in the audience approached me shyly. When she didn't take her eyes off me, I said to her awkwardly,

"Uh, hi. So, what did you think of the meeting?"

"It was great. If it's okay, I'd like to interview you for CHUM radio".

I've never understood why I asked her to marry me, soon after that. I understand even less why she said yes.

Normally, our after-the-fact explanations of key moments in our lives never come close to reflecting what was churning at the time. Sure, I was lonely, as was Judy. But I loved my independence more than anything and I was used to sleeping alone. Perhaps my proposal to Judy was my answer to not being able to have Kathy Denomy. Regardless, I moved into Judy's place a month later.

My IS comrades saw the change in me right away. In his usual manner, Mark Brett took me aside and, well out of Kathy's earshot, he said with a smile,

"You <u>did</u> finally do the dirty deed, didn't you, Kev?"

I smiled back at him awkwardly.

It went deeper than that, of course. I experienced for the first time how intimate love with another grows and flourishes on all the little moments, and how that constant care can bring forth life from where there was none. But such happy absorption also bothered me.

"Do you think it can work?" I asked Kathy Denomy one night after a branch meeting, when, with a slight sadness in her eyes, she'd congratulated me about my engagement to Judy.

"Can we have a married life and still be as devoted to the revolution? Has it worked for you and Mark?".

Kathy's eyes looked even sadder at that point, but she tried to smile as she searched for words. Finally she said,

"You make anything work if you believe in it enough. Just don't try to figure out other people too much, Kev. Especially the ones you love."

The life I had led in Steel City was never the same for me after that. Being with Judy expanded my horizons as well as my heart. I soon felt a longing for something more than being a front-line, full-time Enemy of the State. My natural longing for learning and discourse kindled thoughts of college in me. Judy was on board with me and with any measure that would get her out of southern Ontario and away from her abusive family.

Extracting myself from my political and personal devotion was another matter. Living for revolution had been my reason for being for over five years: a long span of time when you're twenty-two. I knew instinctively that pursuing a career and living for myself and a family was not something that fit my character, and so over time would invite my own destruction.

Knowing that about myself so clearly, why would I bother to get a university degree? Why do anything other than the higher purpose that I knew was the right one?

Besides that, my IS comrades were more than a family to me: they were fellow warriors in a cause that could never be duplicated. People who are joined in battle and who depend on each other for survival can never find the same love or purpose with others. I knew that if I left Hamilton to go to college, I would be leaving behind some of the best part of me. But that is what I chose to do as the year 1979 dawned. And it would take me years to recover that same sacrificial devotion, and at the cost of everything I knew and falsely loved.

My departure from Hamilton was not an easy one. Some of my less-familiar comrades seemed indifferent to my leaving, and my former roommate Barry just shrugged morosely and said,

"So, now you'll build a branch in Vancouver, is that it?"

But Kathy took it hard. She couldn't contain her tears when I broke the news at a branch meeting.

She wished us both happiness, but she and I carefully avoided each other after that, in the manner of those who never forget.

Don Eperson was less gracious about my decision. He had come to depend on me to complete what was the final chapter in his life, and he loved me like a son and a soul brother. We shared a final beer in the Running Pump tavern when his volcano exploded at me.

"Why *Vancouver*, for fuck's sake?" he suddenly spat at me, with venom in his bleary but accusing eyes. He didn't give me time to answer.

"Gone just like that to live off the public tit, like every other fucking student, is that it? Like you're some half-wit prick out to get a law degree and be a fucking parasite somewhere?"

I shook my head and avoided his gaze.

"Well fuck you, you little bastard!" he exclaimed, slamming down his beer glass and making it spill.

"Who the hell needs you?"

Don stood up and cried out bitterly,

"Lots of you fuckers talk about revolution, you know? You talk and you talk. That's all you're ever good for, just fuckin' talk! Well listen to me, you little prick! Talkin' never did nothin'!"

It was the most wounding thing he could have said to me. It was not the best of leavings for two such solid comrades.

But even as Don Eperson turned and walked out of my life, he lodged forever in my heart. For so many times after that he has stood beside me and inspired all my unwinnable battles as no-one else could – especially when all the words have run out.

Chapter Three: From the Campus to the Pulpit

We shall expose the hidden works of darkness and drive falsity to the bottomless pit.
– Peter Annett, *The Free Enquirer*, London, October 9, 1761

Nowadays I feel a lot like Sam Wedge in my novel, watching as his entire world blows away.
– from the diary of Kevin Annett, July 5, 1985

The brutal Somoza dictatorship in Nicaragua was overthrown on the same day that Judy and I arrived in Vancouver. It was July 17, 1979.

As the Sandinista rebels entered Managua and America launched a new global arms race and cold war, I enrolled in an Anthropology undergraduate program on the quiet University of B.C. campus where I'd grown up. Despite the incongruity of those events, I was happy to be home.

None of us who struggled through the 1970's with such a high hope and intention for humanity could have anticipated what was to follow. Like Fred Engels observed, people make history with their eyes on the past.

At that time, the threat of nuclear Armageddon so consciously stoked by the Reagan and Thatcher regimes triggered a Great Fear that struck many of us, making many alleged radicals cautious. While I wasn't touched by that mood, the revolutionary political milieu I was used to began to shrink and I found myself isolated. Former Marxists had become overnight moderates, especially on campuses.

As one of my former comrades declared during that time,

"It just doesn't pay anymore to be too Red."

"Well shit! When has it ever paid?" I replied.

It was fitting that I embarked into academia during the ossifying years of the 1980's. I spent that decade earning three university degrees at UBC: first in Anthropology, then a Master's degree in Political Science after a tentative year in Law, and finally a Master of Divinity degree that led to my ordination as a United Church clergyman in 1990.

I loved the campus as much as the surrounding forests and ocean. At the time UBC hadn't acquired the "Corporate U" spirit of a glorified mall that it now possesses. As when I was a teenager, my happiest moments were spent wandering through the woods and the stacks of the Main Library, where I would settle in for hours to read.

I loved to teach with the same passion. I soon realized that I had found part of my vocation when in 1984 I became a Teaching Assistant during my graduate studies in Political Science. The delight I felt when in a classroom of thirty bored students I found one struggling and searching mind had no parallel in my life. I seemed set on a course that would lead to a professorship, even though such a life felt incomplete to me, a one-dimensional option that didn't answer my silent voice.

But my life then wasn't entirely scholastic. I kept my political oar in the water by helping to launch the Green Party of B.C. and running as a candidate for that party in the 1983 provincial election. That same year, the biggest General Strike in British Columbia history rocked the province. I sat on the campus strike committee that placed picket lines all around UBC. Of course, that meant that I lost two crucial weeks of my first year Law classes, which effectively screwed me at exam time and ended my budding career as a lawyer.

Ultimately, that professional setback didn't bother me too much, considering my growing disgust with the cutthroat culture of the legal fraternity. But I learned a lot about the theory of the law which helped me later.

One of the few rays of light for me in the UBC Law school was an odd duck named Steve Wexler, who taught my Legal Process class. He looked more like a decaying hippie than a professor. On our first day of classes, Steve stood at the podium and smiled ironically at us gaggle of wide-eyed budding advocates and declared,

"It's not against the law for a poor man to starve under a bridge. Comments?"

I was the only one in the lecture hall besides him who was smiling. Everyone else looked confused or worried. My hand shot up.

"That's because the law serves people with money" I exclaimed to the hostile glances of my colleagues. Then Steve and I were off to the races.

The academic world, like the church or any other corporate system, always creates a niche for its token "progressive" figure – especially in Canada.

The game is all about packaging and appearance, since in practice the lip-service radical is just as tightly controlled by the system as everyone else. Steve Wexler, for one, was continually attacking injustices everywhere except on our own campus, and he dutifully ignored the General Strike and crossed our picket lines to get to work. Later, I would encounter the same hypocrisy in spades as a clergyman in the United Church.

As my academic career sputtered and faltered, I fell back on what came naturally to me, as Judy used to say. During those years I helped unionize Fraser Valley farmworkers, fought to save the university forests and created a national coalition to halt the formation of Canada's secret police, the CSIS. But something in me was missing.

During my long, silent walks through the UBC woods I sometimes thought I'd found what was absent. *You've been hungering for this peace, this is what you've been missing!* I'd say to myself, breathing in the damp fecundity of the forest. But my heart told me otherwise: *You are longing for your place at the head of an army once more, standing strong and ready in the essential battle. That is the purpose for which you are made.*

Back then, during my twenties and thirties, I hadn't learned how to take my inner voice seriously and be guided by it, perhaps because I felt that I had so many other things to rely on. I doubt that any of us ever start maturing spiritually without suffering a serious traumatic blow that strips us of who we thought we were.

Nobody willingly chooses radical change, whether in themselves or the world: something I learned the hard way as a revolutionary when I relied on the people around me to choose freedom over security. And so as worldly solutions kept running aground on the hard reefs of my own experience, I was forced to go deeper and seek that inner voice that spoke to me of my essential purpose.

Losing Judy started that process.

Mutual honesty is usually the first thing to go in a romance, and it never ranked that high in our relationship. Both of us avoided the fact that we had come not to love each other, but neither of us would say the obvious. Things drifted that way until our mutual boats lost sight of each other. After seven years together, we finally separated, more from inertia than anything. But the effect on me was profound. I seemed to lose all my moorings.

Things came to a head soon after Judy moved out of our apartment. It was a clear spring day in 1985 and I sought my familiar refuge deep in the quiet of the UBC forest. Despite this tranquility, the struggles and accumulated loneliness of the past decade swept over me like a Tsunami, making everything seem pointless. My inner assurances collapsed. For the first time in my twenty nine years I felt a complete despair, and I fell to the ground like one going under for the final time.

I lay there on the leaves and soggy earth longer than I can remember. Then the sunlight tickled my face and I opened my eyes. On a nearby log a squirrel was eyeing me curiously, an acorn in its tiny claws. The little creature munched sedately and didn't seem at all afraid of me. Then from out of nowhere a majestic blue heron landed gracefully on a nearby tree and preened itself with a similar calmness.

At that moment, the world became harmonious for me. I felt like an atom in a river of eternity. And then everything changed, and I was joined to the perfection. A door opened somewhere inside me all on its own, and I was filled with a peace that was beyond understanding. I felt like I had a new mind and heart. Fear had no place in me.

I rolled over onto my back and let out the boyhood cry of happiness that I used to yell from my ten speed bike as I careened alone along prairie dirt roads. I suddenly knew and owned the truth that had lingered on the margins of my being for so long. I could own my essential purpose.

"The end of one world and the start of another" came a voice in my heart.

I decided that same week to enter the ministry.

………………….

Brighton-Hove Community Radio Station, Brighton, England – June 3, 2010

Interviewer: Well look, Kevin, that must have been quite a jump for you, as a lifelong atheist, to become a Christian clergyman.

Kevin Annett: I guess it might seem that way. It wasn't a burning bush experience for me or anything like that, but don't get me wrong, it was deeply transforming. I suddenly knew there was a deeper purpose for me in life than radical politics or teaching in a college.

You mean a spiritual calling?

If you want to call it that, but I don't. The word's become meaningless from overuse.

Then what's your word for what happened to you?

There isn't one. There's no way to describe to another person what's sacred.

Then you must have had a challenge preaching every Sunday!

Yeah, it sure became more difficult after I ran out of words. That's probably why I opened my pulpit to anyone who wanted to speak.

And that's when the trouble began for you, Kevin.

That's right.

……………………………..

I knew something was wrong when total strangers kept smiling at me.

One of them was a blithe twit who resembled a Young Tory from 1950. He exclaimed at me,

"Welcome! I'm so happy the Lord has brought you here today!"

"Actually, a bus did" I replied. The twit continued to smile at me blankly.

The central rotunda of the Vancouver School of Theology (VST) was crammed with a heap of fresh fish seminarians that morning, ready for the skillet. I felt immediately out of place because I didn't bear the look of impending rapture that everyone else did. But being sufficiently Canadian, I went along with protocol and returned the gesture whenever I was smiled at, which was constantly. After awhile my jaws ached even more than my heart did.

Our warren of pious bunnies was soon channeled into a hall where we were given an official welcome and Pep Talk by the school Principal, a slick talking hustler named Bud Phillips. His words were weirdly like the hype I'd been handed on my first day in UBC Law school: namely, that we special people held the keys to the Kingdom and would prosper in time, provided we played ball, smiled on cue and didn't upset the applecart.

God, apparently, favored us.

Some people noticed my amused smirk as Bud kept prattling on, and their happy grins faltered. Visions from Invasion of the Body Snatchers, of being chased by screaming hordes across the VST grounds, began dancing in my head. *Am I going to make it out of here alive?* I wondered.

Normally I'd have checked out of the entire circus at that point, but there was more than me to consider by then. The previous year I had done what I always told others never to do: I plunged into another relationship while on the rebound from Judy. My new paramour was Anne McNamee, a young Arts student I had met at a "Faith and Justice" meeting on campus. We had wooed briefly, then compulsively married just days before I began my studies for the ministry at VST.

I was remarkably obtuse about people back then. As surely as I should have read the warning signs from the premier burlesque at VST and did not, I encountered the hate-filled stare of Anne's father Jim when I first met him and didn't think it amiss.

Jim was a bitter Irish Catholic who hated seeing his daughter married off to a Protestant pastor-in-training. The fact that he had molested Anne when she was an infant no doubt helped him transfer his guilt-rage onto me. One day his pathology would help fuel the breakup of our marriage and the loss of my two children. But at the time, like all of us, I saw only what I wanted to see.

And so, bemusedly imagining myself as a happily married man on a career fast-track into Christian ministry, I refused to step back from what were the two biggest mistakes of my personal life. One day, fate would use my errors for a better purpose and outcome. But after these past decades of suffering and loss, that silver lining remains cold comfort to me at the best of times.

Anyway, there I was in Christian Munchkin Land. In my state of obliviousness, I was happy enough. Anne started a job in the VST Accounting office the day I began my theology studies, and we moved into a housing co-op near to the campus. I found a part-time job, appropriately enough, at the UBC

Psychiatric Hospital where I hung out with the loonies, including the patients. The insights I gained there of how delusional people operate would one day help me understand the cloud-cuckoo land culture of Christendom and Dumber.

Regardless of my mistakes in life, a hidden hand has always stepped in to slap me hard and get me back on track. And so did it go, soon after my commencement in the strange world of VST.

One evening after work Anne met me at our car in a foul mood. In the manner of any unrecovered trauma victim, she kept her anger to herself. But in the quiet of our home the truth began to surface.

"It's that asshole Bud Phillips" she muttered.

It seems that our Illustrious Principal needed to free up $50,000 from the VST budget to make renovations to his spacious mansion next to the school. Unable to solicit such funds from the senior accountant, Bud had called in all the VST staff and announced that two of them had to be let go. Anne's friend Hanna, a single mom who worked alongside her, was one of those who was chopped. The woman was in hysterics.

After she told me the tale, Anne looked at me with her usual *"Well, so what are you going to do about this shit, Kev?"* look. She always relied on me to be her surrogate conscience. But it's not like I needed much encouragement.

I soon dug into what had happened. It turns out the situation was even worse than Anne imagined. And so, without ado, I issued a leaflet about Bud's sordid maneuver. As with my high school campaign against Limpy Lower, my subversive tract spread quickly through VST as from a mustard seed. It sparked a firestorm among the sedated crowd.

I gave my sardonic edge free rein in the leaflet's title,

"Does Bud's hunger for a Jacuzzi outweigh Hanna's need to feed her kids?".

I tend to credit people – especially those caught in wrongdoing – with more humor and depth than they possess. None of the VST crew laughed at my amused thrusts and jabs at Bud Phillips. In fact, people went hysterical.

In hindsight, those events were a remarkable foreshadowing of the banal madness that fell on me a few years later after I had uncovered and publicized the United Church's much weightier malfeasance against aboriginal children. The usual mask of Niceness among the droll church crowd fell away, and an enraged and snapping beast sprang forward.

Like a demented Captain Queeg, Principal Phillips convened a special assembly of staff and students. Before the quaking crowd Bud demanded to know who had issued the leaflet.

Not even the more liberal VST faculty took offence at this sudden descent into McCarthyite frenzy. They too glared inquisitorially at our assembled student body, probing for the malefactor. I was tempted to get up and challenge Phillips for what he was doing. But the moment passed, and Bud and I soon parted unsatisfied.

The bastard got his renovations, naturally, but at the cost of his image. People looked at Principal Bud differently after that. The criminal still held royal power but even his minions were aware now of some of his nakedness.

As for yours truly, no-one discovered the identity of the mysterious author of the leaflet. Nevertheless, I remained a prime suspect in the minds of the Pharisees, as became evident from the general shunning I subsequently experienced at VST and my unfair treatment during exams and my final round of Ordination interviews.

The fiasco helped prepare me, in a perverse sort of way, for my next kick in the ass by Vested Interest. It all started, strangely enough, in my Greek and Hebrew class.

My Hebrew professor was a visiting lecturer named Harry. He was friends with a Guatemalan refugee named Enrique Torres. Every year, Enrique took groups of Christians on "fact finding tours" of the refugee camps strung along the war-ravaged southern Mexican border. Knowing my political bent, Harry suggested my name to Enrique, and we soon met up.

Enrique had barely escaped from his country alive in 1981, one step ahead of a death squad. He had been the lawyer for the workers at a Coca Cola plant, and that corporation hired killers to squash their union. Most of its leaders were killed, but

Enrique and his family made it to Vancouver. He saw my social justice passion right away and asked me to sign up for the next tour of the Guatemalan refugee camps, set for the following month.

Anne didn't like the idea of me heading south into a war zone, but I assured her that my participation in the trip would improve my standing in church circles, which placated her a bit. The United Church was big on human rights for natives in Guatemala at the time, which was absurdly ironic, considering how the same church has led the slaughter of Indian children across Canada and still traffics them. And so, somewhat Kafkaesquely, in April of 1987 I journeyed with Enrique Torres and five other Christian Do-Gooders to Chiapas, Mexico.

After surviving the rigors and madness of Mexico City – my lungs nearly packed it in from the smog and my heart from the legions of starving, begging children – we arrived in an opposite world: the mountainous jungle near Tuxtla Gutierrez, from where we bussed to the refugee camps. As the forests gave way to dry and barren plains, the first of dozens of camps came into view, crammed with thousands of Mayan Indians who had fled over the border from a rampaging Guatemalan army. Our destination was a squalid settlement called Nueva Esperansa, which means New Hope.

Our guide was a short, bearded guy with a quirky smile named Fidel, which means Faithful. He was a defrocked catholic priest who lived and worked with the refugees. He met us at the gate, but a swarm of dozens of thin and sickly children had beat him there. The young ones eagerly grabbed our hands, laughing and jabbering away in their native Quiche tongue.

"They're mostly orphans" Fidel remarked after we'd been introduced, gesturing to the children.

"Their parents were caught in the recent massacre at Aquacate. We try to keep them alive but they're dying, some quicker than others."

I quietly followed him as he led us into the camp. The squalor and stench were beyond belief. Young men bearing antiquated rifles stood guard along the way, staring at us with hard, calculating eyes.

"We can't grow crops here, so we bring in food and water and everything else from the outside" explained Fidel.

"Every month we lose another hundred children from dysentery, typhus and malnutrition. But these people are amazing, they've endured everything, and they stay together as a community. They've fought invaders for centuries and survived. The Quiche have a saying: *They have cut off our branches, but they will never destroy our roots.*"

"What are their roots?" I asked him, as Enrique interpreted.

"They are the roots, themselves. They don't speak of God or a Creator, they talk of the immortal spirit of the earth and how the people are a part of it."

During our days in the camp, Fidel came and went a lot, and he sometimes went into hiding. I learned later that his assassination had been ordered by a local wealthy landowner who did not liked his "revolutionary" sermons. Two years later, the killers finally caught up to Fidel, thanks to the local Catholic Bishop who was a friend of the landowner. The gunmen shot Fidel nine times. A thousand Mayan Indians came to his funeral.

Although I didn't know about the hit that had been ordered on him, I asked Fidel at one point if he was ever afraid about being there. He nodded and stared at me with his solemn brown eyes, replying,

"When I get scared and I want to run away, I go and look at the poorest children in the camp and I remember that they can't escape from here. So, since they can't, why should I?"

The children followed us everywhere. One little boy with rickets grabbed me by the hand the first day I arrived and led me to the shack where he and two dozen other people lived. Everyone wanted me to sit down and eat with them as they shared the little food they had, mostly dried out tortillas. As one of them said to me through an interpreter,

"People call us poor. But our leaders are always the poorest ones among us because they work every day and night for the people. The true leader serves others and never thinks of himself."

I had never been among people who loved each other the way the Quiche Indians did. They would die for one another, and they did every day. All that I knew in Canada seemed barren and lifeless in comparison. I felt that I was the one who was impoverished and dying, not the Quiche.

This fact was demonstrated at our last evening in the camp, at a dinner held in our honor. As we fat gringos sat down to eat, I saw that on our plates, alongside the mainstay of black beans and tortillas, was a small pile of scrambled eggs. The Quiche had given us their best food, the few eggs in their camp, as was their ancient custom.

I was shocked. I looked at the lean and starving faces of the children around me and offered the plate of food to the nearest ones. But Enrique grabbed my arm and said sternly,

"Don't insult them. Eat it."

And I did so, honoring the Quiche on their terms. But it was the body of Christ on which I fed. It was the Quiche people, given to me so that I may live, in ways still unimagined.

Fidel was watching me closely. He could see that my struggle was not only about eating the best food while the children hungered in front of me. He seemed to sense the deeper crisis building in me, and the choice that I would have to make one day: the same one Fidel had made, at the eventual cost of his own life.

It was a perfectly true moment, stark naked in its agony and triumph. Later, seeing the change working in me, Fidel shared a story.

"It took the Quiche a lot of years, but they finally turned me into a Christian. I tried teaching the Indians about the sacraments, but they knew better than me! The communion wafers vanished from our chapel one day. It turns out the Quiche had been sharing them with their friends in the jungle, the streams and the trees and the animals. They said that God was in all creatures so how could we not share communion with them? That was enough to get me defrocked by the Bishop. But that didn't matter because I'd already been ordained by the people."

Fidel's happy words lodged in me as firmly as did the Christ-presence of the Quiche. Pregnant with the miracle and pondering it in my deepest heart, I returned to the shadow world of VST and what called itself the Church. But the miracle of Chiapas would soon come back to take flesh in me and lead me to my own Golgotha.

....

It happened soon after that, as it was meant to.

Her name was Kathleen Teare. She was twenty-one years old and turning tricks along Main street when I first met her. Churning with something other than compassion, I stopped and picked her up.

Without much ado, the young woman offered to help me relieve myself for twenty bucks. I gave her the money but declined the service, suggesting instead that I drive her home.

"You've got to meet my Mom" said Kathleen, her embarrassment slackening the more we talked.

"She's a real angel but way down on her luck. She needs help."

The place was destitute by Canadian standards. As I picked my way through various heaps of rubbish, an older woman's voice spoke weakly from within the dark slum apartment.

"Oh no Katie, you shouldn't have brought anyone here …"

"It's okay Ma, I think he's someone who'll help" Kathleen replied.

The woman was thin and sickly. She stood shakily and averted her eyes as I extended my hand.

"I'm sorry we're like this" she said nervously.

Her name was Margaret Teare. For years she had been a psychiatric nurse who relied on uppers and downers to get her through her split twelve-hour shifts. Eventually heroin took over and she and her husband Colin became heavy users. They blew through their savings on drugs and ended up unemployed and on welfare.

As I stared at both Margaret and Colin, who lay unconscious on a couch, I could see the demon was visibly sucking them both dry. But something else was at work. I felt it the moment Margaret looked me squarely in the eyes, and I knew I was facing an angel.

It had been six months since I had been welcomed by the Quiche people and their everyday divinity, but in an instant with the Teares, I felt the same unfettered love and acceptance. When I touched hands with Margaret, I experienced as I had in the refugee camp a spiritual family more real than any I knew.

Margaret's mouth fell open as she looked at me. Tears came to her eyes.

"You've been sent to us!" she exclaimed.

"You're a man of God, come to be our minister! You've come for people like us, just like Jesus did."

She had spoken my heart perfectly. And her words bestowed on me my calling more truly than did my ordination by the United Church two years later.

I spent a lot of time with the Teares after that. I brought them food and they fed my heart. I knew instinctively that their presence formed a spiritual counterweight and antidote to the soul-numbing meat grinder I was being put through at VST and in the church. I was in my second year at seminary by then and the choice that Fidel and the Quiche had kindled in me was looming. Margaret was my mentor and midwife through that spiritual birth.

"You're too good for the church" Margaret often said to me, as I shared with her the moral void that I had to navigate each day. But Margaret saw more clearly than me where things were heading.

"You're one of Christ's own, Kevin, so the church people will hate you and try to destroy you."

Despite Margaret's accurate prophecy of my future and her plea for me to stay clear of organized religion, Anne and I were attending First United Church by then, in the heart of Vancouver's skid row known as the Downtown East Side. I sat on the church board, ran its community outreach, and had my first taste of street ministry and of preaching. My premier sermon culminated in a brawl when two street guys in the pews went after each other, ironically, just as I was waxing fervently on Jesus' call to love our enemies.

Then as now, the impoverished neighbourhood is not so different than most, except that everything is visible, as in any internment camp. The dealing and the whoring go on day and night in a mad and grasping frenzy of greed, as if the animus of our entire mammon culture has crystalized and taken flesh in the ten-block radius of the Downtown East Side. Maybe that's why the place is such a magnet to the wealthy Johns from the west side who flock there at night in their SUV's with the inevitable baby chair in the back seat. Everything and anyone in that world can be bought, used and conveniently discarded; or so it seems.

What became my new home is, like the Quiche refugee camp, a ghetto of poor people under a lethal attack. As I write these words, hundreds of homeless people in the Downtown East side have vanished as part of the cop-run "COVID Cleanup". Mass disappearances are not a new thing in the neighbourhood. No homeless person is allowed to cross the line into the plush downtown core or the outlying suburbs. The cops make sure of that, usually through rapes, beatings, or Midnight Rides from which a lot of men and women never return.

In the same way, the Vancouver police allow drug dealing and crime to flourish in the neighbourhood so that local property values will plummet, and the place can be bought up cheaply by the governing offshore real estate moguls. The same cops also play a big role in the local drug trade on behalf of its Chinese Triad crime overlords by covering the incoming shipments at the waterfront docks and scaring or killing off small time competitors.

I often demonstrated this collusion to Do-Gooder visitors by showing them how the Triad-approved drug dealers ply their trade on the very doorstep of the police station on Main street without ever being hassled by the cops. The visitors never got my point, no doubt because they didn't want to.

The longer I worked along East Hastings street and its murky environs, the more I began to meet the survivors of our homegrown Holocaust. Thousands of aboriginals struggle for survival there, many of them after being forced off their land or reservation by implacable multinational companies and their bought and paid for tribal council chiefs. And nearly all the street Indians endured the slaughter called Indian residential schools, where half the children never survived.

One of the witnesses to that slaughter was Johnny Dawson, who everyone called Bingo. I met him early on, since he was hard to avoid: he perched rain or shine in an alcove at the corner of Main and Hastings. He was a Nishga Indian from northern BC who as a boy did three years of hard time in the Anglican prison called the Alert Bay Indian school.

"I finally broke outta there before they could take my balls" he told me once, and eventually explained what he meant.

Bingo knew everything that went on in the 'hood, and once we got to know each other he was my gateway to many other residential school survivors who had a lot to tell me. Crouching next to Bingo and listening to their horror stories was a continual kick to my head.

"See Maggie over there?" Bingo said to me one evening, gesturing at an intoxicated native woman.

"I knew her at Alert Bay. They had her on the oven detail. And I don't mean she was baking bread."

Bingo paused and puffed on a joint thoughtfully before continuing.

"The young girls there got raped and pregnant from the priests, all the time. So, they'd take the newborns and toss 'em in the oven, alive. She had to do it, or she'd be dead. If she talks about it now she'll be dead."

While they lived, Bingo and Maggie and those like them shattered the world I knew. As my ordination in the ministry approached, I occupied two contrary worlds, the official and the actual: the Canada I thought I knew, and a nation of bloodshed and lies.

This split was presaged by the culture shock I'd received in southern Mexico but working on skid row made the dichotomy intensify. For I learned quickly that Crimes against Humanity in Canada were not a thing of the past. Murder, torture, child trafficking and human snuff films were all occurring just blocks from where we conducted our snug Sunday services at First United Church. Unable to keep the worlds separated, I tried speaking about what I knew in our congregation and my theology classes at VST. That was a bad idea, at least for career conscious clergy.

To take one example, during a Pastoral Care course involving how to deal with abuse victims, I tried to share my experience of Shirley Roberts, a single mother on welfare to whom I was bringing food. The woman's three-year-old daughter Amber was acting out all the signs of severe sexual abuse. I soon discovered that Shirley was pimping out Amber to her neighbours in return for drug money. I told Family Services and the police, but neither agency did anything. Somehow Shirley caught wind that I knew of her shit and quickly disappeared with Amber.

As I spoke, my classmates and teacher stared at me dumbstruck. The professor promptly announced that my example was "not appropriate" to the class discussion. I replied,

"But our course topic is about victims of abuse, isn't it?"

The prof never answered me. And after that I became even more of a pariah around VST.

Like something concocted by a trickster deity, my estrangement continued during my final year at VST and the final round of ordination interviews that would determine if I had the "right stuff" to be a United Church clergyman. The schism continued until it finally snapped and overturned my world and the world, according to a purpose still unseen.

But before that happened, I underwent an even greater enigma: I became a father.

....

The night was blanketed by a snowfall-imposed silence that was punctuated only by the sound of my footsteps and the toboggan I dragged. My two-year-old daughter Clare lay on the sled, almost indiscernible within her bundled clothing, watching me and the snow with her calm, blue-eyed gaze.

I stopped briefly to marvel at the prairie quiet and the wonder of the moment. Remarkably, the only sound I heard came from the impact of countless icy snowflakes on the earth. Clare smiled up at me and let out a delighted little giggle.

Our home by then was in Pierson, Manitoba, population 321, where I pastored my first church; three churches, in fact, scattered over forty miles of farmland. Suddenly I found myself reveling in the unexpected delights of my firstborn child and a steady job. The schism in me seemed to rest for awhile. I knew somehow that my personal joy would not last, for I had awoken to an evil with which I would one day contend. But for the moment, Clare's smile, Anne's satisfaction and my undemanding daily routine as a country pastor seemed enough for me, even when it wasn't.

My parishioners made it easy for me to imagine staying among them and raising my family there. They were uncommonly decent and basic people but utterly limited, concerned with nothing beyond their farm and their families. I envied them in their contentment. But I already knew that my purpose lay elsewhere.

Still, our year among them showered both heart and memory with golden moments, especially involving Clare. She sprouted each day in front of us like good wheat, delighting not only her parents but the elderly ladies in our church who cuddled her and passed her around the pews all during worship. One night, Clare stumbled into my office bearing a chocolate cookie she had baked with her mom, extending its half-eaten piece to me with a messy smile and outstretched arms, uttering her favourite phrase, "Daddy, up!".

Our prairie idyll ended when a job posting in street ministry opened in Toronto. I applied, and out of forty candidates I was unanimously chosen for the position. And so, late in the summer of 1991 we said our goodbyes to my parishioners and made our move. The first Gulf War had just begun to slaughter thousands of people, and many children.

Our destination was called Fred Victor Mission: the United Church's biggest urban project in Canada. I was hired to develop an Urban Ministry presence there among the homeless and the residents of its low-income housing unit on Queen street. I didn't realize, nor was I told, what a nest of corruption, criminality and hidden agendas I was walking into. But that's the church for you.

One of the first people I met at the Mission was Mike Burca. He was a street guy who hung around the Drop In and who claimed to be a former secret policeman and bodyguard for the former Rumanian dictator Nicolae Ceaușescu. He said to me candidly,

"Don't trust anybody in here. This place makes my country look like paradise."

Mike was not exaggerating. A few months later, when the shit began hitting the fan because of my work, he showed me computer records from the Mission. They revealed that more than a million dollars had gone missing and that millions more were unexplainably appearing in the accounts. To my quizzical look he replied,

"It's money laundering. I've seen it before."

Mike was a good man with a gentle heart. He often joined me on my nightly walkabouts to tend the homeless. But he was targeted because of what he knew about the big money and underworld ties to the Mission. Before I was fired without cause by the Mission's top honchos, Mike Burca disappeared one day and was never seen again.

During my time at the Mission, I became a magnet for people like Mike since I was always available and accessible. Anyone with a grudge or some dirt on the church approached me, whether I was conducting worship services, walking the streets, or visiting folks in the rabbit cages called Mission apartments. But as I learned later in Port Alberni when I helped to surface deeper church crimes, my openness to people and willingness to go to bat for them was like lighting a match in a room full of dynamite. What I was learning from the local people was almost beyond belief.

My biggest revelations came from my nightly street walks, when I circulated among the homeless folks who slept in the local loading docks and dumpsters, and on the hot air grates around Toronto City Hall. A particularly cold winter had fallen on us and people began dying from the cold, including men and women who I knew and who attended our worship services.

One night in December, Mike and I encountered a heap of seven Indians sleeping on the City Hall hot air grates. They were covered in snow and mostly asleep. I offered coffee and soup to one of them who was awake, an old Cree man. As he sipped, he told me they had walked three hundred miles in the snow to escape their northern reservation.

"Why?" I asked him.

"The Chief tried killing us to get our land. He sells it off to Ontario Hydro. We got to stay outta sight 'cause if the cops find out we're here they'll do the job on us to get the bounty."

I asked him if they'd tried sleeping in the all-night shelter run by the Catholics. The old man snorted.

"You crazy? Those fuckers raped and killed my little sister when she was four. They still sell our kids outta St. Mike's, just down the street."

By the new year of 1992, the open circle worship I held at the Mission was filling with people like the old Cree man. People were voicing allegations of wrongdoing and violence in the neighbourhood, including by Mission staff. I never tried censoring anything people said. The result was inevitable.

Soon the word began to percolate up to the United Church head office that a meddlesome clergyman at Fred Victor was digging where he shouldn't.

I was still stupid back then, and so I thought I should write to the United Church Moderator about what I was hearing. Early in February I set down all the allegations in a letter to Walter Farquharson and other top church officials. I never got a reply from any of them. But the following week I heard from Fred Victor Mission Director Paul Webb, who called me into his office. He was furious.

"It looks like you've been taken in by a lot of lies and wild rumors being spread about our work here" Paul exclaimed, his chubby jowls shaking. I was perplexed.

"You mean in my letter to the Moderator? You've seen it?"

Webb continued to fume,

"I can tell you right now that our financial records are as clean as a whistle. And it's not true that drugs are being dealt here by the staff or that prostitution is going on in the Mission housing."

"I hadn't heard that last one, actually" I said impishly.

Paul turned a bright red. Then he said coldly,

"Kevin, it's like this. An urban ministry position has come up at the Sherbrooke Street Center. It's just like your present job and it even pays a bit more. I suggest you apply there."

Somewhat dumbfounded, I answered,

"But I like my work here. We've started up a street church and the people depend on me."

"This is a one time offer" Paul Webb interrupted angrily.

"I can't predict what might happen to you. If I were you, I'd think of your young family."

Things began to come apart quickly after that. The next day I got a message to report to someone named Paul Mills, who was the Chairman of the Fred Victor Mission Board. His address turned out to be a lavish Bay street law office overlooking Lake Ontario. It had a view perhaps not dissimilar to the one that accompanied the offering of Three Temptations.

Mr. Mills was all business. Without even rising to greet me he barked,

"Have you written to anyone else about your claims?"

"What, you mean about the drug dealing, the money laundering ..." I began.

"Have you sent your letter to the media?"

I shook my head in confusion.

"Are you the one making such claims or are there others?".

Feeling like I was on a witness stand, I hesitated. He stared at me with seasoned, dead eyes for a moment and finally said,

"Look, Kevin, we know all about those things going on at Fred Victor. The only problem here is that you wrote a letter about it."

He couldn't have summed up the situation better or proven to me more clearly that the perpetrators never have to worry about implicating themselves over things they don't consider to be a crime.

But Paul Mills had it wrong. The problem was not my letter; it was that I still didn't know what I was a part of, and what was really in charge of it. That special knowledge would dawn on me only after my next encounter with the crime calling itself the United Church of Canada, in a lumber mill town called Port Alberni in British Columbia.

Chapter Four: The Slaughter of the Innocents

Then he kicked her. She went rolling down the stairs. She wasn't moving, she wasn't breathing. I see that all the time.
– Harriett Nahanee, eyewitness to the murder of Maisie Shaw at the Alberni Indian Residential School, December 24, 1946

Kevin had this coming to him.
– United Church official Phil Spencer after Kevin Annett's firing without cause, Port Alberni, January 25, 1995

Once again, my little family was on the road. This time we were heading west in the middle of winter, pregnant with not only our second daughter Elinor but the seed of something explosive.

I was fired without cause from my job at the Fred Victor Mission soon after my revealing encounter with Paul Mills. In response, I immediately applied for United Church postings on the west coast, where both our families lived. We hoped to settle there before Elinor's birth that summer. But my fate continued to pursue me, even among the familiar pleasantries of the west coast.

Little did I know that even before we arrived there, a negative report about me had been sent by Fred Victor Director Paul Webb to United Church official Art Anderson of the United Church's head office in Vancouver. The letter scurrilously blackened my name, castigating me as an incompetent employee and "someone to watch". Three years later, the same Mr. Anderson fired me without cause from my new posting and helped scuttle my life.

Despite this backroom subterfuge, my applications for work struck pay dirt immediately. A struggling congregation in Port Alberni caught my interest. After a brief job interview, the search committee of St. Andrew's United Church unanimously chose me as their new minister. And so, just a week after my daughter Elinor was birthed rapturously into my arms, the four of us moved to Port Alberni to begin a new life. It was July of 1992.

As hopeful as I was at the time, a dark foreboding touched me the first time I drove into the fog-shrouded Alberni valley for my job interview. If I had followed my feelings I would have turned around and never come back. Something unseen and lethal lay coiled in that land. Only later would I know it for what it is.

I caught a whiff of that hidden malevolence on my first Sunday at St. Andrew's church. During coffee hour, as I learned peoples' names and engaged in the usual after-service chit-chat, I was approached by Fred Bishop, the chairman of my church board. Fred was a former mayor in town whose family had been among the first white settlers in the Alberni valley in the 1860's. They had arrived soon after a convenient smallpox plague had wiped out most of the local Indians.

Fred smiled slightly as he said,

"That was a good start today, Kevin, and a fine sermon. It looks like we made the right choice for our minister."

I thanked him and then asked something I'd been musing about all morning.

"You know Fred, I've heard that many of the local Indians are baptized with us. So, I was wondering why none of them were in church today."

The old guy looked surprised. He grew sober and said with undisguised annoyance,

"They keep to themselves just like we keep to ourselves. Everybody likes it that way."

Later that week, someone unexpected answered my question to Fred Bishop: an Indian, in fact. His name was Danny Gus.

Danny was a retired local fisherman who wanted to finally marry his long-time partner Clothilda. He rang me up and asked me if I would perform the service in their home on the Tseshaht reservation. Eager to meet some Indians, I quickly agreed.

I didn't know at the time that Danny and Clothilda's home stood right next to the grounds of the former Alberni Indian residential school that was run by the United Church for almost a half century, until 1973.

After the service, Danny and I sat in his living room sipping tea and chowed down on chummis, which is salmon eggs in oil, and tastes as bad as it sounds. Danny kept tapping his pipe and gazing out the window at the grounds of the former school. Finally I asked him the same thing I'd queried Fred Bishop about.

The Indian didn't say anything for awhile. He was obviously struggling with something. Eventually Danny lay down his pipe and looked me squarely and sadly in the eyes.

"The United Church people killed my best friend up there in that residential school. They beat him to death and buried him in those hills out back. That's why we don't go to their churches and that's why they don't want us in them."

....

The storm-swept land fronts on the Pacific Ocean and gives the people their name Ahousahts, which means "Those who face the sea". There are only a few thousand of them left alive now, when once they numbered thirty times that, before the Great White Plague.

None of the Ahousahts can remember much about their origins or the calamity that arrived in sailing ships off their coast in 1770. Their nation was all but exterminated in barely two generations. And the fallout of that deliberate genocide endures to the present day.

I began to meet some of the Ahousaht people and the other remnant native bands during my first weeks in the Alberni valley. They were not hard to miss since they comprised a third of the local population. But like most Indians in Canada they keep to the shadows, especially in their own minds. Those of them who live in town are as walled in by an official silence as they are by the slums that they occupy in what is still known as The Ghetto.

When the cluster of aged white folks hired me to "bring new blood" into their dwindling congregation of St. Andrew's, none of them told me what my young family and I would be walking into. Small wonder. The year I arrived, Port Alberni had the second highest rate of unemployment, poverty, family violence and drug-alcohol abuse of any municipality in B.C. The valley seethed with anger. It was the only place I had been where drivers consistently changed lanes to run over seagulls. The violence among the Indians was even more extreme: something I learned when I began to routinely conduct the funerals of teenaged aboriginals who had killed themselves or babies found dead and bruised in their cribs.

The most basic and obvious question to ask was what was responsible for this war.

Unfortunately, nobody wanted to even pose that question. When I began speaking about our community ills in my sermons, people looked away and some even gave me hate stares. The locals seemed to be harboring a terrible secret that no-one would dare mention.

Despite this grim secrecy, the very fact that I was addressing it inspired others in the valley. The weekly attendance in my church began to grow. Within six months I had tripled our numbers and the pews were filled on Sundays. Some of the new people were aboriginals, and their numbers grew after I opened our Loaves and Fishes food bank in the church basement. For the first time in local history, white people were seated alongside natives in church. That mixing was tolerated at first, but one day it became explosive.

Events in the outer world were adding to the maelstrom. The year after I arrived, the biggest protest in local history exploded not far from us in the Clayoquot Sound, over the fight to stop the clear-cutting of the last old growth cedar forests.

Many of the people in our pews were involved in that battle on both sides of the line, as loggers and environmentalists. Often on Sunday mornings my open pulpit policy would cause the voices of bitter opposition to ring out through our sanctuary, to be followed by everyone joining hands and praying together to find our common ground. This example of unity despite our differences was not lost on the Indians present, and encouraged them to speak from the same pulpit with a devastating truth.

Alfred Keitlah broke the ice. As the patriarch of the first aboriginal family to start attending my church, Alfred stood up one Sunday during worship and began speaking a prayer in his native tongue. His aged, trembling voice that echoed through the sanctuary seemed to awaken spirits that had long been silenced.

More voices from the pews quickly followed from his example:

"They killed my baby Charlie at the hospital last month. They wouldn't treat him for his cough and they just sent us home. They said Indians got to go to the reservation for help." (Karen Connerley)

"Before your people came to our land your Christ came to my people and told us to welcome the white strangers because they were sick and lost and had only some of his teachings and had forgotten the important ones, about respect and equality. We are still welcoming you, but you have much to answer for and much to give back to our people." (Nelson Keitlah)

"Our purpose given to us by Creator was to guard the forests, the rivers and the animals of this land. To steal all that the whites had to make us forget who we were. That's why they brainwashed us in their residential schools, and they killed those of us who wouldn't go along." (Earl Maquinna George)

"I think it's super cool the way anybody can stand up in this church and say what they think without fear. I've never seen anything like it. I just wonder how long it's going to be allowed to carry on." (Mark Angus)

The crushed truth that was gradually standing up and speaking in my congregation represented the worse crime in Canadian history, and the most concealed.

A quarter century later – now that it is fashionable and safer to speak of genocide in Canada since the criminals of Church and State have been legally absolved and indemnified - the horror and depth of the crime is still beyond the grasp of Canadians. It was equally denied by most of my parishioners when it was first named in my Port Alberni church.

The fury of the final extermination of indigenous nations was concentrated on Canada's west coast between the onset of the Gold Rush in 1868 and 1920, when the native population had fallen to barely one percent of its pre-Conquest level. At this nadir, when 20,000 coastal Indians were left alive out of two million original people, the misnamed "Indian residential school" system was created under the joint management of Church and State, by a governmental Order in Council. The aim of that system was to complete the destruction of the remnant Indian groups and create a new, "aboriginal" populace of compliant slaves.

That genocidal purpose succeeded beyond the wildest hopes of the invaders. And it still governs the thing we call Canada.

But the special horror of the Canadian genocide is that it has targeted and been perpetrated against children.

Over 60,000 boys and girls died in the so-called Indian residential schools: nearly half of those who were incarcerated there. That death rate, which even government records and the stage-managed "Truth and Reconciliation Commission" admits, was higher than the mortality rate of the African slave trade and the death camp of Auschwitz.

This abominable fact has never seemed to bother most Canadians, even when the detailed evidence of the crime was painstakingly surfaced and presented by me and a few others for over two decades, following my Port Alberni years.

When children were starved, gang raped, sterilized, tortured and worked or beaten to death by "people of God", consistently and legally for over a century, no level of official Canadian society ever raised a word of protest: even when the enormous death rate was reported in national newspapers as early as November, 1907.

"None of those bastards who worked in there *(the Alberni residential school)* were human. They didn't care who they killed, and they still don't" recalled my friend Harry Wilson, who was one of the first survivors to go public in the spring of 1997.

The Indians whose voices first echoed in my church in the spring of 1993 were the last ones standing from this enormous slaughter, and their truth has faded with each passing year. But at the time, the impact of their voices was beyond measure, in our community and eventually across the nation.

Many of my non-aboriginal parishioners listened to these new voices, and some of them even tried to understand them. But a hard rump of parishioners refused to and began to actively undermine what had sprung up among us like an unplanned growth. This rump included Fred Bishop and four others, all of whom had worked in the United Church's Alberni residential school and who hated the fact that Indians were in the pews. One of these opponents was the daughter of the clergyman Alfred Caldwell, who according to eyewitnesses killed two native children while Principal of the Alberni and Ahousaht residential schools.

And yet despite this, even the oppositional rump was not untouched by the new spirit moving among us.

On one memorable Sunday in the fall of 1993, after I had baptized an aboriginal baby and walked him around the church so that everyone could greet him, our most diehard racist, Ed Spencer, began to stiffen as we approached. So I made a point of standing in front of Ed and holding the baby up to him. Suddenly his frown softened, and his eyes began to moisten. His were not the only ones that shed tears that morning in our church.

Sadly, the men who caused the axe to fall on our burgeoning revolution were not present and susceptible to the cleansing innocence of a baby. The wheels had already been set in motion to smash all that we were building, and my life in the process.

During my first year at St. Andrew's, Fred Bishop met with church officials Art Anderson and Bill Howie. Along with some local Presbytery officials, they began to secretly monitor my work and gather alleged "dirt" that could be the pretext used to eventually get rid of me.

Before the axe fell, the full depth of the residential schools nightmare had not been uttered by the aboriginal voices among us, despite my open pulpit policy. Like in any healing circle, the worst pain remained unspoken at first, as people tested each other and themselves. But even their muted voices aroused the wrath of the guilty.

I learned of the storm that was gathering from one of my best friends in the church, a young man named Mark Angus. Mark was someone of constant devotion and goodness. He was a mainstay of our food bank and often went with me to the two local Indian reservations to hold prayer services and distribute food. He helped me launch a city- wide group known as LIFT (Low Income Folks Together), that campaigned for affordable housing and jobs. Mark was the one who wondered aloud in a church service how long our experiment in truth telling would survive before it would be shut down.

Early in January of 1994, Mark came to me in a troubled state. He had caught wind of a campaign to remove me as St. Andrew's minister.

Mark claimed that the plot against me involved "bigger people" than just our church's old guard. I could see that something deeper had him spooked. But Mark didn't want to say anything else until we had relocated to a safer place.

He took awhile to respond after we finally settled on a nearby park bench. His voice was low and anxious, and his eyes kept glancing around.

"There's people who want you dead, Kev. I mean big money people, they're real gangsters, the guys who bring in the drugs from offshore and who traffic the native kids. I know half the Mounties in town, and I've heard their scuttlebutt. If they can't boot you out of your job, they're going to take you out for good. You've got to believe me!"

I had recently received a few anonymous death threats, so his words didn't completely surprise me. But I kept my silence as Mark continued.

"I've got to tell you all this because I don't have much time left. I know too much of their shit and they know it. I've been stupid, mouthing off to the wrong people. But I'm not worried about me, it's you I'm afraid for. You're the one it hates, you're the one it wants to destroy …"

"What do you mean by 'it', Mark?" I interjected.

He gave a slight shudder and shook his head.

"You don't know what you're up against, Kev. The evil thing that's killed all those kids, it's hiding behind religion, it's hiding in our own church. It hates that you're pulling off its mask and exposing it, and it wants you dead. You don't see it, you're too good and trusting with people, even the ones who are trying to wipe you out. But you can't trust anyone now, not even your wife. You're going to be totally alone. You'll only have God on your side."

More clearly than anyone, Mark Angus saw the truth of what we faced and what was to befall me. Perhaps for that reason he was found dead a week later in a nearby hotel room. As with many of my friends who have been killed for knowing too much, Mark's death was ruled a suicide. That edict was issued by the city's coroner, Gillian Trumper, who was close friends with Fred Bishop and who one day became the Mayor of Port Alberni.

Mark's death snapped the manacle of fear that had tried fastening itself around me. I began to talk to my parishioners more about what I knew, starting at Mark's funeral and similar services I conducted for other murdered members of my church, like Krista Lynn and John Sargent.* And in the fall of 1994, just a few months before I was summarily fired from my pulpit, my supporters in Port Alberni began to plan a "Peoples' Tribunal" to investigate local crimes against native people.

That Tribunal never convened, for the hammer of repression began to fall hard on anyone in the Alberni valley who was a supporter of mine. Even before my firing on January 23, 1995, aboriginal church members were threatened and scared off, and a public smear campaign against me began. The writing was clearly on the wall.

....

* Krista and John were also members of our LIFT group who shortly before their deaths had publicly accused the local RCMP of raping and killing native women and trafficking children off the Opetchesaht and Tseshaht reservations. Both of them died of alleged drug overdoses even though neither of them were drug users.

Despite this escalation of our battle, a quiet before the storm descended on my family and me. My daughters Clare and Elinor were five and two years old by then. I often took them with me on my visits to parishioners or to the local Indian reservations, where they would watch wide-eyed at the swarms of ill-clad and hungry children their own age. Clare, being older and more aware, sensed the raised sword over my head. One night she came into my office at home and asked me how much longer we would be living there. I didn't know what to say.

Despite a heartening vote of approval for my work by over 90% of my parishioners at our fall church retreat, forces I couldn't imagine were planning a devastating assault against us. Mark Angus had warned me of what was to come. And now I would face the cataclysm alone, with only an obscure God and my own will and courage to rely on.

Chapter Five: Under Fire in the Land of No-One

We had no trouble with Kevin until he wrote his letter about the Ahousaht land deal. A senior government official told me, "We can't have Kevin upset the applecart over Lot 363".
– Win Stokes, Comox-Nanaimo Presbytery official, September 3, 1996

Kevin Annett had no future in our Department after he started writing his thesis about the Alberni Indian residential school.
– University of BC Educational Studies faculty member Murray Elliott, June 2, 1998

The blow that ended my life and began a new one fell on October 19, 1994. On that day Marion Best, the Moderator of the United Church of Canada, began the process that would see me fired without cause, defrocked without due process, stripped of my employability and children, and forced into poverty and a permanent national blacklisting.

Marion did not act alone, but in collusion with John Cashore, another United Church cleric and a cabinet minister in the BC government, and with the secret church committee set up by Fred Bishop and Art Anderson the previous year.

What prompted their rapid move against me was a letter to church officers I had written on October 17, 1994, which served as the pretext for their action. Addressed to the Comox-Nanaimo Presbytery, it objected to the theft and sale by our United Church of land belonging to the Ahousaht people, known as Lot 363. I urged that our church's standing policy be enforced and that we freely return the land to the Ahousaht people.

In my "Mr. Smith Goes to Washington" naivety, what I didn't know at the time was that the same piece of land was part of the biggest and most secret corporate takeover in the history of British Columbia: the buying of MacMillan-Bloedel, which was a major funder of the United Church, by the American logging corporation Weyerhauser Ltd. My letter threatened to "upset the applecart" (in John Cashore's words) by exposing the secret deal and how the church, companies and B.C. government (which was the largest shareholder in MacMillan-Bloedel) were profiteers in stolen native land and genocide.

In short, a certain meddlesome Port Alberni pastor had to go. Official policy on native land rights is one thing, but big money is what calls the shots – especially in the United Church of Canada.

The October 19 decision was a green light to everyone who had an axe to grind against me and the changes I was unleashing in the Alberni valley. That included the congregational faction around Fred Bishop, the unholy trinity of church, state and corporate big shots who were directly threatened by my exposure of their Ahousaht land deal, and other clergy in our Comox-Nanaimo Presbytery who were incited against me by Anderson and the others. Two of these ministers, Foster Freed and Phil ("Kevin has this coming to him") Spencer, subsequently led the move to have me removed and defrocked without the knowledge of anyone in my parish or the Presbytery.

One night just before my firing, I received a phone call from Fred Bishop. He told me that the congregation was "upset" at my work and wanted me out. I was shocked. I asked him how that could be when I had just received an overwhelming vote of support at the church retreat.

Ignoring my remark, Bishop declared that I could keep my job as minister only if I did three things: close the church food bank that was feeding over two hundred families, stop preaching about social justice and bar "non-members" – his term for Indians - from our church services. I declined, reminding him that he did not have the authority to make such a demand on me. But Fred Bishop remained adamant.

Even more shockingly, my wife Anne McNamee took part in this plan to expel me. For over a year, she had been involved in an illicit affair with a local cop named Joe Pistotnik. Art Anderson and Phil Spencer had found out about the affair as well as Anne's counselling sessions concerning her childhood rape by her father Jim. The church men approached Anne with a blackmail-offer: if she cooperated with them to get rid of me, she would win custody of our daughters in any divorce action. The United Church would also help her financially in resettling if she left me. If she didn't play ball with them, the church would make sure that the world found out about her childhood abuse and her involvement with Joe Pistotnik.

Anne quickly agreed to cooperate with Anderson, Spencer and the other plotters. The fact of this collusion surfaced during our subsequent divorce trial, which sure enough granted Anne full custody of Clare and Elinor, despite the proven violence and rape within her family of origin.

The national United Church office also took part in this criminal conspiracy. During 1996 alone, the church's central office through its "Mission and Service Fund" paid at least $26,000 to Anne's Vancouver divorce lawyer, Ron Huinink: something that Huinink and Anne both admitted.

This multidirectional assault on me began on January 23, 1995. On that day I was fired without cause by Art Anderson and threatened in writing with permanent defrocking from my profession if I didn't agree to a "psychiatric assessment" and a year long retraining without pay. These were unwarranted demands designed to discredit and scapegoat me, as the church later admitted. Their aim was to distract attention from their crimes of child murder and land theft that I was unearthing by "shooting the messenger".

This criminal conspiracy proceeded on schedule quickly. Every attempt I made to negotiate with the church and work out a resolution was sabotaged by church officials, who were determined to expel me under as odious a cloud as possible. I was blocked by Comox-Nanaimo Presbytery from applying for other positions in the United Church. Rumors were circulated within my congregation that I had become "mentally unstable". My family and I were ordered to vacate the manse where we lived, even though our daughter Clare was in kindergarten and it was mid-winter. By the summer we were forced to move away from the Alberni valley and resettle at Anne's parents' house in south Surrey.

Making that move was personally heartbreaking for me, since it compelled me to abandon my work and community. But it was also a proverbial jump from a frying pan into a fire, since Anne's father Jim was secretly working with the church to plan the impending divorce trial against me. And yet still in shock by my firing and fogged by my own good will, I couldn't see the breadth of my enemy's aim, or the depths to which they would sink.

Many in my church were outraged at first by what was happening to me, especially after our church food bank was shut down and my supporters were barred from Sunday services. But their anger and wishes weighed little in the balance. The national church office ordered them to comply with my firing, and most of them did.

Not everyone stood by in silence or complicity. Some of the natives in our church led by a feisty Metis named Jack McDonald started picketing St. Andrew's church on Sunday mornings, demanding my reinstatement. They also called for a criminal investigation into the church for genocide. But when two of these protesters, Krista Lynn and John Sargent, were found dead in their apartments, my supporters fell away. The point had been made: if you strike the shepherd, the sheep will scatter.

Jack McDonald was one of the few people who did not retreat in the months after my firing. During the funeral that I conducted for Krista Lynn – who shortly before her death had publicly accused the United Church of "crucifying Kevin" and the RCMP of killing native women – Jack stood up to speak.

His words helped set my course over the years that followed.

"Kevin got axed by the United Church for the same reason they killed Krista Lynn: because they're trying to hide the genocide they did to our people. We know the names of the men who killed children up at the local residential school. They're still trafficking children off the reservations. It's up to us to put those killers on trial. It's high time we held a Peoples' Tribunal to do exactly that."

Thus inspired, Jack and I launched the movement that would one day force a criminal Church and State to admit genocide and would even bring down a Pope.

The church had its spies at Krista's funeral, and they quickly counterattacked. Two days after Jack spoke, United Church officials Brian Thorpe and Art Anderson met with my wife Anne and paid her to start divorce proceedings against me, as she had agreed to do. Their plan was to hit me with a two-fold divorce and defrocking punch at Christmas. But an unforeseen incident upset their sordid arrangement.

Her name was Harriett Nahanee.

By that time, in the late fall of 1995, I was still blocked from working anywhere in the Church. And so after resettling in Vancouver, I had enrolled in a doctoral program in Educational Studies at the University of BC, where our family was ensconced in student housing. My story had made the rounds in the local activist community, and new supporters were holding protests at United Churches about my firing and the bigger issue of Indian residential school crimes. At one such action where I was present, outside the United Church head office in Vancouver, a bedraggled aboriginal woman named Harriett Nahanee showed up bearing a sign that read, *"I saw a child get killed at the Alberni residential school."*

Harriett was just eleven years old on Christmas eve, 1946 when she saw Principal Alfred Caldwell murder Maisie Shaw. Hiding under the stairs of the girls' dormitory at the Alberni Indian residential school, Harriett heard little Maisie crying for her mother. Caldwell began screaming at her and in Harriett's words,

"Then he kicked her. She went rolling down the stairs. She just lay there. She wasn't moving, she wasn't breathing. I see that all the time."

Fortunately for posterity, a Vancouver Sun reporter was on hand at our protest, and Harriett's account of the killing hit the press the next day under the headline *"Claim of Murder goes back fifty years"*. It was the first time the Canadian media had reported the killing of a child in an Indian residential school. The date was December 18, 1995.

Two days later, a second eyewitness, Archie Frank, reported another killing by Alfred Caldwell: that of Albert Gray, age 9, at the United Church's Ahousat Indian school. The Sun article was entitled *"Beaten to death for theft of a prune."*

The killers in robes reacted as if they had been hit by a cattle prod, and they exposed themselves in the process. A national press release was quickly issued from the United Church's head office that claimed no knowledge of the deaths of these children. The release then contradicted itself by saying that that no attempt had been made by their church to conceal those deaths, even though no-one had yet accused them of a cover-up!

At the same time, the church privately ordered its BC Conference office to immediately begin my defrocking. That same week, with the church's prompting, Anne announced she was divorcing me.

But it was all too late. Soon after, the first lawsuit was launched in the BC Supreme Court by Alberni Indian residential school survivors against the United Church and the federal government. It was the first court action of its kind. It opened the litigation floodgates and changed Canada forever.

....

It was an odd time and an unexpected way for me to turn forty.

Even as the life I had known was being destroyed, I was experiencing the exhilaration of igniting a firestorm of change across the country. But that movement was not apparent right away and took years of struggle to manifest. Even when it did, it provided cold comfort when stacked against the enormity of suffering inflicted on not only me and my children but a lot of people who posed a threat to the criminals in power.

Prompted by her United Church handlers, my wife Anne dropped her calculated bombshell on me on Christmas eve. In front of our two daughters, who were still only three and six years old, she announced that she was divorcing me.

As I struggled with my own tears and those of my children, who went hysterical in response to their mother's words, I saw with horror that Anne was smiling.

The truest definition of human evil I have found is that which deliberately inflicts destruction on the innocent. I have encountered that darkness in many forms and among friends and strangers, but I never expected to grapple with it in my own family as it tried to destroy my children. Whatever the entity was that acted through Anne's crazed, possessed mind cared nothing for the trauma that its actions were unleashing. Its demonic aim was to create maximum pain and confusion in me to incapacitate me and make me unable to pull back its mask any further.

Evil notwithstanding, this is the standard method of eliminating whistle blowers, by first destroying the ones closest to them.

During this period, I experienced in a dramatic way that there was a power at work in the destruction of our family that was greater and more malevolent than a simple marital breakdown.

Soon after Anne announced that she was divorcing me, I tried to mend things with the gift of an Eagle feather that had been used in healing ceremonies among the downtown natives with whom I was working. I approached Anne from behind with the feather, intending to give it to her and say a prayer. But before I could reach her or she had even seen the feather, she leapt up as if I had given her an electric shock and screamed in a coarse and unfamiliar voice,

"Get that thing away from me!".

Having participated in three spiritual exorcisms, I know that such a reaction is a standard symptom of demonic possession. Anne's continued aberrant behaviour bore out this prognosis. And the rampant destructiveness of this Entity continued to play itself out through the people it possessed; especially the Christians.

Mark Angus had been completely accurate when he saw how the entity's corrupting spirit was hiding itself within religion. But even Mark may have been astonished at the totality of its grip on those who did all they could to destroy my life and that of so many others over the years that followed.

Early in the new year of 1996, Anne disappeared one night with both my daughters, after receiving the go-ahead from Brian Thorpe. The next day, having slept not a wink, I was served with her divorce papers.

In her court application, Anne demanded full custody of Clare and Elinor as well as crushing support payments from me that I couldn't afford. In barely a fortnight she won it all, thanks to two compliant Family Court judges who fast tracked her case and didn't bother with any inconvenient facts. On April 4, I was ordered out of my home, and I never again saw my daughters on a full-time basis.

Just two days later, I was notified by the United Church that I faced permanent defrocking as a minister at an upcoming "delisting" hearing that would be chaired by none other than Jon Jessiman:

the same church lawyer who had secretly arranged my firing and the theft of my children.

In the same vein, during the week when Family Court was deliberating on Anne's custody claim, Brian Thorpe clinched the deal by having a close personal friend of his, Vancouver Sun reporter Doug Todd, publish a lie about me in the form of an article entitled *"Fired minister ordered to take psychiatric test"*. In fact, the church had already dropped their demand that I take such a test, admitting that they had only used it to hasten my removal. But Todd's slanderous piece did its job, and the children went to Anne.

"Conflict of interest" is as foreign a concept to an Inquisition as is due process or the rule of law.

In hindsight, the savagery of these coordinated attacks made sense, in a twisted sort of way. The United Church was by then in full damage-control hysteria and reacting with a scatter-gun approach to the hundreds of personal injury lawsuits from their former residential school students that began sweeping the country. They must have figured that wiping me out would somehow bury the issue.

Fortunately, that was not to be. Events were on my side. The Canadian press was not yet domesticated on the issue of the Indian residential schools and continued to report new horror stories from the survivors that I was feeding them.

In response, and sinking to new levels of duplicity, the three guilty churches – Catholic and Anglican, besides the United – began lying to the world by claiming in the press that they faced financial ruin from the mounting lawsuits. But as I quipped with reporters who were routinely calling me up for my comments,

"Those churches are already morally bankrupt, so why shouldn't they be financially?".

Part of my cockiness came from the fact that, even as my life was being torn apart, through my studies I was uncovering a tremendous new weapon for my arsenal: archived microfilmed documents in the UBC library that proved the guilt of both Church and State for their Indian residential school crimes. Some of those documents would soon prove pivotal in the historic court cases that made the churches' guilt not only undeniable but a legal fact.

In the manner of the hidden hand that has guided me, I was led to this material almost accidentally.

Early in my doctoral program, I was privy to a conversation among my fellow students referring to the "RG 10 material" recently acquired by the UBC Koerner Library. The RG 10 designation referred to federal Department of Indian Affairs material from British Columbia Indian residential schools between 1890 and 1965: a cornucopia of school and health records, official correspondence, and even reports of the deaths of students. None of this priceless material was held anywhere else in Canada.

I had hit the mother lode.

Over the next several years I practically lived in the basement of Koerner Library, poring through the hundreds of files that illuminated the buried history of the Christian death camps that Canadians still call Indian residential schools. I quickly began to publish these records and speak about them in media interviews. In doing so I added fuel to the growing fire that was sweeping the aboriginal world, as residential school survivors stepped forward for the first time to name crimes almost beyond belief, and to sue the churches in court.

Over time, many of the RG 10 documents proved invaluable in not only the courtrooms but the healing circles for survivors to which I began to be invited, as word of my firing and discoveries spread through the "moccasin telegraph".

One example stands out.

Early on in my research, I uncovered in the files of the Koerner Library a document known as the Application for Admission Form: something every native parent had to sign, or they would go to jail. By signing it, the parents surrendered their legal guardianship over their children to the Principal of the residential school, who was invariably a church employee. The churches therefore had no basis to claim that they were not fully responsible and legally liable for the fate and damages done to the incarcerated children in the so-called residential schools.

This document was indeed a bombshell, for it destroyed the entire legal defense of the mainline churches: namely, that the government and not they were ultimately responsible for the crime.

After I gave copies of this crucial document to the lawyers for the Alberni school plaintiffs and they introduced it in court, it served as the basis of the historic Brenner Decision in the BC Supreme Court in June of 1998. That decision found the Canadian government and United Church "equally liable" for the "institutionalized pedophilia" *(sic)* at the Alberni Indian residential school.

On an even more human level, I personally witnessed the power of sharing the Application for Admission Form with residential school survivors.

For their entire lives, many of these men and women had been unable to overcome their shame and hatred of their parents for not rescuing them from the hellholes where the law placed them when they were as young as three years old. Whenever I showed the survivors the Form and explained how it had legally robbed them from their families and handcuffed their parents, a weight seemed to lift from them, especially after we would ceremonially burn a copy of the Form in the fire.

The truth, indeed, began to set the victims free.

The churches that were responsible for the death and suffering of so many knew this all too well, as their panic visibly increased the more that I made such documents public. The hysteria of the church drones became comical on more than one occasion.

In June of 1996, my friends and I were staging a protest and press conference on the steps of the United Church's head office in Vancouver. I quickly distributed copies of the Application for Admission Form to the plentiful reporters who were there that day. I also announced that because the church was proven to be legally liable for the deaths of so many students, they should be charged with crimes against humanity in Canadian and international courts. The press ate it all up.

Little did I know that the same two men who had orchestrated my firing, defrocking and divorce – Brian Thorpe and Jon Jessiman – were peering at our action through an upstairs window. Without my knowledge, Thorpe snuck outside and stole a bundle of my documents out of my briefcase that lay behind me.

Fortunately, someone caught the theft on film.

"Hey Kev, that church guy just ripped you off!" said Caleb Sigurgierson, the student who'd filmed it.

A troop of us, including reporters, quickly walked upstairs and confronted Jessiman and Thorpe, who was frantically trying to photocopy my material. Upon seeing our crowd, he tried hiding the pages behind his back.

I took great delight in declaring to Thorpe as the TV cameras whirled,

"Brian, I'd like the documents you stole returned to me, please".

"I didn't!" he blurted out, edging away from me.

"Is this joker really the CEO for the United Church in BC?" Caleb said incredulously, as even the reporters laughed.

A red-faced Jon Jessiman suddenly barked at his minion,

"It doesn't matter Brian, just give it back to him".

Thorpe did so sheepishly. Then the rest of us left the building, in triumph and mirth.

After the incident didn't make the evening news, unsurprisingly, I realized that I needed to charge Brian Thorpe with theft. I figured it was a slam-dunk case since the incident was caught on film. But I was about to receive another lesson in Canadian realpolitik.

I went to the Vancouver police with my charge, but they referred me to someone named Garth Gibson, who was a Crown Counsel. In the standard manner of British-style colonialism, the police in BC don't lay charges; only the Crown Counsel does. And the latter is the personal appointee of the provincial Attorney-General; namely, the party in power.

When I finally caught up with the elusive Mr. Gibson after nearly five months of unreturned phone calls and door knockings, and I insisted that he charge Thorpe and Jessiman with theft, the Crown Counsel was not amused.

"It's not in the public interest to pursue this" Garth said to me curtly after I had confronted him in the main hall of the provincial law courts.

"Why not?" I said.

No answer.

"But it is a clear case of theft, isn't it?"

"Yes" he said cautiously.

"Well then?"

No answer. I continued,

"This theft is also a matter of public and legal interest, namely the deaths of aboriginal children."

Silence. I said to Mr. Stone Face,

"Look, is there someone else I can talk to about this?"

"No, there isn't"

"Why not?" I asked him.

"Because I'm the one who decides what's in the public interest"

"Just you?"

"That's correct"

After a pause, I said to him with a smirk,

"You aren't a member of the United Church by any chance, are you?"

Garth Gibson walked away with hatred in his eyes.

This tag-team coverup arrangement between State and Church is as old as smallpox blankets and so is still in operation across Canada. But despite this, there arose during those many years of struggle something the arrangement could not contain: the combined power of documentation and testimonies of eyewitnesses to lay bare institutional criminality, whether in the courts of law or public opinion.

But Rome wasn't sacked in a day. The few of us who dared to unite the written and eye-witnessed proof of mass murder in Canada during those years faced the full wrath of the malefactors, and few of us survived it.

This David and Goliath battle took many years. But the more I began to surface the documents and witnesses of church crimes, the more determined became my former employers to crush me for good. And so, amidst my first discoveries, protests and press conferences, the deadly duo of Thorpe and Jessiman commenced the kangaroo court that would fraudulently expel me from United Church ministry.

....

Reverend Annett's request to know the charges against him is out of order. How many times do I have to say that?
– Jon Jessiman, Judicial Adviser to the Conference "Delisting" Trial of Kevin Annett, August 29, 1996

I doubt that in our rage at him about all his social justice stuff, we would ever have given Kevin a fair hearing.
– Bob Stiven, former Chairman of Comox-Nanaimo Presbytery, October 3, 1996

Someone who still cares advised me recently that I was a masochistic idiot to have endured the six months of stage-managed abuse and illegality by the United Church that posed as a legitimate hearing into my "eligibility for ministry". That is certainly the view from the sidelines because, of course, my critic wasn't there.

What brings light must endure burning, observed Victor Frankl. The more the official machinery of an unaccountable church tried igniting the flames on my funeral pyre, the greater was illuminated its own fraudulence and filth. That was the silver lining on the farce of my public defrocking as a minister.

The pathetic kangaroo court that destroyed my livelihood occurred between August 1996 and March 1997. Its details are sublimely absurd and perhaps unbelievable to the uninformed or the naïve. But this all happened. I know because I was there:

A judge who has lunch with the prosecutor and the jury during the trial.

A defendant who cannot know the charges against him, the names of his accusers or the rules under which he is being tried.

The denial to the defendant of the right to call witnesses, examine evidence or consult the court record: rights granted to the prosecution.

Evidence against the defendant that he cannot see, and which has been solicited by the prosecutor during the trial.

A judge who consistently rejects the defendant's request for due process and to know the charges against him on the grounds that such a request is "out of order and disruptive".

The allowing of hearsay and innuendo about the defendant to be entered as evidence by the prosecution.

A judge who makes prejudicial remarks about the defendant on record, including "We've come to expect this from him" and "He's created this problem for himself."

A judge who before the trial advised others to fire and discredit the defendant, who blocked attempts to resolve differences with him, and who was complicit in the theft of the defendant's belongings and the ruination of his family and reputation.

For any reader who is alarmed that such a gross miscarriage of justice could occur in Canada in recent years, be advised that such methods are the norms of secret church hearings, which, like the Star Chamber courts of medieval Europe, know nothing of the rule of law. For centuries, church Inquisitions have operated from the same basic principle: that the church is always right, and the defendant is always wrong.

As the Attorney General of BC, Ujjal Dosanjh (who was a personal friend and a cabinet colleague of my nemesis John Cashore) described in a letter to twenty-two people who attended my defrocking trial and demanded that he intervene to halt its injustices,

"The internal procedures of the United Church of Canada are outside the jurisdiction of this department".

That is, the United Church is outside the laws of Canada.

So there in print, the province's top legal officer confirmed what I learned the hard way: that the Church is a law unto itself. That fact explains the ease of my railroading out of my profession. But it also accounts for how the same church legally murdered tens of thousands of native children with the help of the Canadian courts and Parliament.

The subject of Indians, especially dead ones, was of course carefully excluded from the agenda of my defrocking by my Inquisitors, who claimed to be evaluating my work as a minister. That seemed odd not only to me but to the observers present, since my ministry with aboriginals had been a cornerstone of my work in Port Alberni and led directly to my firing, especially after I challenged the Church over its theft and sale of the Ahousahts' traditional land. The truth was that it was precisely over the matter of dead little Indians that I was being expelled from the church.

The fact that I was also the first minister in United Church history to be *publicly* defrocked also struck people and the press as something more than significant. As a retired cop who sat in on some of the hearing observed later,

"Who ever washes their dirty laundry in public unless they're making an example of somebody? And who spends over $300,000 to do it and boot out one minister? The whole thing had 'show trial' written all over it."

To add absurdity to the entire spectacle, the Three Stooges who comprised the delisting panel that would decide my fate as a clergyman were all personal associates of Jon Jessiman, who was the judge of the hearing despite having engineered my firing and divorce. The panel members had been selected by Brian Thorpe, Jon's partner in crime.

The head Stooge, Mollie Williams, had even nominated Jessiman for United Church Moderator and was a friend of his family.

The lawyer who conducted the "case" against me on behalf of the church, Iain Benson, was an odd little guy. A virulently right-wing Catholic, Benson took personal delight in trying to nail me. He was forever on the verge of exploding in unprovoked rage at me. Maybe Iain's anger was due to the fact that he didn't earn the more than $50,000 he was paid by the United Church for his efforts, since he never proved that I was unfit for ministry, which was the whole point of the exercise.

Of course, none of that ultimately mattered. I was defrocked anyway.

In his hubris and hatred, Iain Benson exposed the absurdity of the hearing with some quite startling admissions, including one of my favorites,

"We have said repeatedly that there are no charges against Reverend Annett, that he faces no disciplinary action and that he did nothing wrong. Nevertheless, he is not fit for United Church ministry."

Their charade was supposed to slam-dunk me in a week, but it dragged out over six months because I fought their miscarrying of justice at every step. I kept asking for the charges against me and they were never given. I asked for hard evidence that I wasn't a competent minister, pointing out that I had filled the pews of St. Andrew's church and kept them full until the day I was fired without cause: a fact that contradicted the church's claim that I had severely "alienated" my congregation. But actual documented facts didn't impress the panel as much as disparaging rumor and innuendo about me.

The only "witnesses" called to testify against me had either rarely or never met me. When I tried to call my own witnesses from among people who had seen my work firsthand, I was prevented.

Amazingly, Jessiman specifically forbade during the hearing any reference to aboriginal people, Indian residential schools or the Ahousaht land deal. Of course, much to his chagrin, I discussed those things anyway. Whenever I did, Jessiman signaled to the court reporter to not record anything that I was saying!

Heard enough? I certainly had, after a month of no due process and such gross bias and illegality. But I persisted in my efforts, inviting in the press and witnesses. I knew that only thus could the farce be placed on the public record and demonstrate the criminality of the church and the conspiracy that had engineered my destruction.

Comically, proof of that plot dropped unexpectedly from the mouth of a Comox-Nanaimo Presbytery official named Win Stokes, whose handling by Iain Benson was something less than expert. When Stokes was on the witness stand, Benson opened the door to the issue that from his perspective he should have avoided like the plague, which was whether I had been fired unjustly.

Stokes was a guilt-ridden man: a relatively honest guy who had been bludgeoned into being a front man for Jessiman, Thorpe and John Cashore. He clearly didn't enjoy being there or covering for his guilty associates. So, in a panicked attempt to distance himself from the sordid plots surrounding my firing, Stokes blurted out in response to Iain Benson,

"We never had a problem with Kevin until he wrote that letter about Lot 363 in Ahousaht. Then it was decided he had to go. I mean, well, a senior government official told me to my face that we couldn't have Kevin Annett upset the applecart over Lot 363, there was just too much at stake."

At that point, both Benson and Jessiman shared a common look of horror, no doubt because Stokes had referred to provincial Aboriginal Affairs minister John Cashore, who had instigated my firing from St. Andrew's. Jessiman immediately dismissed Win Stokes from the witness stand and ordered that his statement be stricken from the record.

The outcome of the hearing was a fait accompli from the start, as twenty-two witnesses described in their fruitless letters of protest to Attorney-General Ujjal Dosanjh.

"A failed attempt at cosmetics"; "nothing but a witch-hunt from start to finish"; "a not very subtle hammering of an inconvenient pastor": these were some of the comments of the observers. But their voices went unheeded.

On March 7, 1997, the Made-to Order verdict was announced. On that day, I was "delisted" as a minister of the United Church of Canada. The decision was permanent and could not be reviewed or appealed.

The same day, a lawyer for the church, one G.R. Schmitt of Ferguson Gifford law firm in Vancouver, issued a Cease and Desist letter against me that threatened to sue me if I ever spoke of the details of either the Ahousaht land grab or my delisting.

I made a point of ignoring their threat and spoke out publicly about everything. In the years since then I have never been sued, either by the United Church or any of the people I have officially named for their crimes against children. That should tell you a lot. And yet the United Church's lies about both me and their fraudulent hearing still stand as official gospel on their website, or whenever my name comes up in their incestuous circle.

As someone once observed, it takes only a few people to commit a crime but an entire community to conceal it.

....

He went into a rage when he saw the newspaper article about you, Kevin, and he demanded that I remove it from my office door. He told me that you had no future in our department, that you were a terrible husband and father and were telling lies about his church. I felt in fear for my own safety. I pray that you will be careful because this professor has destroyed other grad students he doesn't like.
– University of BC Doctoral candidate Helen Papuni in an email to Kevin Annett concerning the actions of faculty member Murray Elliott, April 3, 1998

The quiet forests and libraries of the university had been my sanctuary since I was a teenager, and they didn't fail me during these years of torment.

After my firing by the church, I had instinctively returned to the campus. Even before the divorce, I had applied to a Ph.D. program in the Educational Studies Department at UBC. My thesis research and class time provided a counterweight to insanity as Anne left me, I lost my children and I ran the defrocking and blacklisting gauntlet of the United Church. But the long arm of genocidal Church and State reached into my burgeoning academic life and snuffed it out as well.

As I described earlier, during my studies I came across an invaluable resource of microfilmed documents from the west coast Indian residential schools that spanned nearly a century. Revealingly, whether now or early in 1996 when I discovered the RG 10 files in Koerner Library, no-one but me has ever analyzed and published this goldmine of evidence concerning the real conditions in the "schools". The simple reason for this is that the RG 10 material blows apart the official narrative that has been crafted by the guilty. Consequently, this evidence is still banned from publication or use across Canada, especially in libraries and the curricula of schools and colleges.

I first experienced this extreme censorship soon after I began to share some of the more damning RG 10 documents in my post-graduate seminars at UBC.

Early in 1997 I shared with the other students a copy of the official record of the enormous death rates in the early Indian residential schools chronicled by two government doctors, George Orton and Peter Bryce.

"You'll notice that a forty to sixty percent death rate among the children began almost immediately when the schools opened in the 1890's, and continued for the next half century" I explained, as I handed out copies of the doctors' reports to my colleagues.

"You should also notice the remark by Dr. Bryce when he said, *'I believe the conditions are being deliberately created to spread infectious disease. This is a national crime.'* "

Everyone looked confused. The seminar instructor, an officially approved "expert" on Indian residential schools named Jean Barman, voiced the general concern by replying with a frown,

"*Deliberately* created? So, what are you saying, Kevin? That these deaths weren't accidental?"

"Well, isn't that obvious?" I said, asking her,

"How can so many children have died constantly over so many years unless it <u>was</u> intentional? Wouldn't the death rates have fallen if the school authorities were taking preventive measures? Bryce said the children who were sick were being deliberately forced to sleep with the healthy kids.

And then less than a year after Bryce's report he got fired and all medical inspection was officially abolished in every residential school."

A long, tense silence followed my words. I knew I had gone far to prove intentional genocide. But the truth is never the issue with many people as much as career prospects and pension plans. Embodying the whole country, Jean Barman turned away and said nothing more to me. The other students did the same.

The flak started soon after that.

Don Wilson, a genial professor who had agreed enthusiastically to be the chairman of my thesis committee, told me sheepishly that he couldn't do so any longer, without saying why. The head of my Department, Patricia Vertinsky, called me into her office and told me that I needed a more "balanced" approach in my research into the United Church's Alberni residential school. She then placed faculty member Murray Elliott onto my thesis committee, even though he had no background in Indian education and "just so happened" to be sitting on the very United Church body that was deciding whether to defrock me.

Conflict of interest, anyone? Apparently not, in the mind of the university administration.

I had never met Murray Elliott, but he knew all "about" me. As he sat on my thesis committee, he was bad-mouthing me all over the Department and smashing my academic freedom into little pieces.

According to Helen Papuni, another student, Murray called me names to her face, said I would never complete my thesis and demanded that she remove a favourable newspaper article about me from her office door. She warned me to be careful, that Murray has trashed other students before me.

Helen was right on point. Within a few months, Murray Elliott had blocked any academic funding for me, despite my first-class standing, and had discouraged other faculty from working with me. Unable to pay my tuition, I was forced to drop out of the program. And the censorship of me on the UBC campus continued, blocking me from giving lectures even when invited to do so by faculty. As recently as the spring of 2019, UBC scholars who quoted my work found themselves censured and reprimanded.

Even though by then, in the spring of 1998, I found myself forced out of another profession by the United Church, I nevertheless held in my hands invaluable dynamite that in a just world and a genuine court of law would have blown apart the bloodstained churches and government of Canada. So instead of publishing my research as a thesis that would gather dust on a library shelf, I shared my evidence with the world: at press conferences, at native healing circles, and in flyers handed out to church goers. The cyclone had begun.

Within a year, the movement that I had launched would begin to overturn the world.

Chapter Six: Turning the Tables on Caesar

Representatives from the International Human Rights Association of American Minorities (IHRAAM) were in Vancouver earlier this month to investigate allegations from survivors of Indian residential schools in B.C. Those who spoke during the IHRAAM forum stated they had witnessed murder, rape, sexual molestation, routine beatings, and electric shocks to five-year-old children who misbehaved. They also said that young women were involuntarily sterilized, and abortions were induced in pregnant girls. A report accompanied by 19 hours of videotape testimony will be presented to UN Human Rights Commissioner Mary Robinson on July 31 in London, England, said Kevin Annett, a former United Church minister and adviser to IHRAAM.

– from "Probe of Canadian residential schools to be reported at UN" by Robert Matas, *The Globe and Mail*, June 20, 1998.

Today the federal government announced a limited program of compensation for Indian residential school survivors who can prove they suffered harm in the schools. The Aboriginal Healing Fund's compensation package requires that survivors legally indemnify the alleged perpetrators before receiving any money.

– from "Indian School survivors to get compensated" *The Canadian Press*, January 18, 2000

Representatives of Mayan indigenous groups condemned Canada today at the United Nations and in a formal 'denuncia' or protest to the Canadian government for its alleged 'genocide' of indigenous children ... The denuncia requires that Canada show proof that it is prosecuting war crimes within its own borders or face possible international sanctions.

– from "Mayan Indians attack Canada" in <u>Global Perspectives</u>, London, December 29, 2004

As many as half of the aboriginal children who attended the early years of residential schools died of tuberculosis, despite repeated warnings to the federal government.

– from "Natives died in droves as Ottawa ignored warnings" by Bill Curry and Karen Howlett, *<u>The Globe and Mail</u>*, April 24, 2007

Thirty-five native people and their supporters calling themselves The Friends and Relatives of the Disappeared occupied the Vancouver offices of Indian Residential Schools Resolution Canada on Friday. The group is threatening an 'escalating campaign of civil disobedience' to force the government and churches to return the remains of the more than 50,000 children they claimed died in the schools.

- from "Native group threatens trouble" in *<u>24 Hour News</u>*, May 24, 2007

The Friends and Relatives of the Disappeared, a group representing a segment of residential school survivors, is preparing to take the federal government to international criminal court and disinter the bodies of native children ... 'We need a genuine war crimes court with the power to subpoena and prosecute the churches and Canadian government' said Kevin Annett, a group spokesperson.
– from "Native group warns of international court action" by Jorge Barrera in *The National Post*, February 13, 2008

Two dozen native protestors stormed the Easter services at Vancouver's Roman Catholic cathedral yesterday demanding to know where the bodies of children who died in residential schools are located. The Friends and Relatives of the Disappeared served an eviction notice on the church, saying it is a squatter on native land ... Similar occupations and evictions have occurred this past week at United and Anglican churches across the country.
– from "Native protestors disrupt Easter services in Vancouver" by Jeremy Hainsworth, *The Globe and Mail*, March 24, 2008

In an historic ceremony in The House of Commons today, Prime Minister Stephen Harper issued a formal apology to former students at the Indian residential schools for what he termed 'a long history of abuse,

neglect and disregard for the lives of First Nations
children.' Other party leaders echoed the Prime Minister
and called for a more thorough investigation into the
fate of the missing children … Bloc Quebecois leader
Gilles Duceppe spoke of 'mass graves' and compared
residential schools to Nazi death camps.
– from "Government apologizes for Indian residential
schools", *The Canadian Press*, Ottawa, July 8, 2008

The freedom I felt after being expelled from UBC
and yet another career path was like the relief that
accompanied my earlier firing from the toxic
environs of National Steel Car. I was out on my ass
but at least I could breathe again. Academia is as
stifling and controlled a culture as the church, and
despite the uncertainty of how I would now support
myself, I was glad to be free of it. Now I could
share what I knew with the world, and especially
with the Indian residential school survivors who
would benefit the most from my research.

I started doing so immediately alongside Harriett
Nahanee, the eyewitness to Maisie Shaw's murder
whom I had met at my church protest a few years
earlier.

Early in 1998, Harriett asked me to help organize a weekly circle of residential school survivors at the Carnegie Centre in Vancouver's downtown east side. Soon, the circle's participants started talking about more than just their personal suffering and recovery.

Picking up on Jack McDonald's idea from my Port Alberni days, I proposed that we hold a Tribunal into the crimes we were documenting, and publicly place the churches and feds on trial for genocide. Some of the survivors loved the idea, and others were terrified. A group of us took the first steps.

We started on February 11, 1998 by holding for the first time in Canada a Public Forum on "The Indian Residential Schools Genocide". The response was tremendous. Over six hundred people showed up to our meeting, which was held at the Simon Fraser University campus in downtown Vancouver. Most of those present were aboriginal and included many survivors. The speakers were Harriett Nahanee, two Alberni school eyewitnesses to murder, Harry Wilson and Dennis Tallio, and me.

To an alternatively hushed and weeping audience, Harriett recounted how she had witnessed Maisie's murder on Christmas Eve. Harry and Dennis both described finding the dead bodies of children on the grounds of the Alberni school. And I provided a lot of background about the unknown history of the "schools" that I had gleaned from my research. But an unexpected speaker from the audience stole the spotlight that evening.

Her name was Marion MacFarlane. She was a white woman who had worked as a matron at the Alberni Indian residential school in 1963. In her words,

"I only worked there six months before they fired me. I would have quit anyway. I couldn't stand all the beatings and late-night burials going on, it was totally inhuman. But what clinched it was when I knocked cold one of the other matrons who was beating a little Indian girl to death with a piano leg. Because then the Principal, John Andrews, sacked me, not her. He said anything that happened to the 'little squaw' would have been better than firing that woman because she played the organ in their church on Sundays."

Harry Wilson added to her account.

"That Principal John Andrews, he locked me up after I found the dead girl's body. I found her next to the school, she was naked and covered in blood. She was a Haida girl I knew. I ran and told Mr. Andrews and the next thing I knew he locked me up in the Nanaimo Indian Hospital. I stayed in there for months, they gave me electric shocks to the head to shut me up about the girl."

These stories and news of our event spread rapidly through the Canadian media. The government and churches kept silent on the matter, even when questioned. They were on the defensive and caught off guard by our actions. The number of lawsuits began to increase, as did the witnesses who were speaking out.

Our initiative had sparked a fire that spread quickly across the country because we were the first people to speak publicly about these atrocities. In so doing, we were filling a political vacuum created by the fear of the "official" (*read: government funded*) aboriginal leaders to raise the issue of Indian residential schools. In fact, they had been explicitly ordered by their government paymasters not to do so.

A crop of these brown puppet politicians perched warily in the front row during our February 11 public meeting. They and the other state-funded chiefs remained as silent and impassive during that time as the government and the churches, besides issuing a press statement that called for a vague "disclosure" from the government. The latter was being wrongly portrayed by the press as the main culprit in the crime. All our mounting evidence pointed instead to the churches as the instigator and force behind the Canadian Holocaust.

News of our work soon spread abroad. Barely one week after our forum, an aboriginal human rights group known as IHRAAM sent a field worker named Rudy James to meet Harriett Nahanee and me, and some of the eyewitnesses. A Tlingit Indian from Alaska, Rudy pulled no punches.

"If a tenth of what you've documented is true, then Canada and these churches need to be charged at the United Nations with genocide."

And thereafter was born the first formal inquiry into Canadian Indian residential school crimes. The vision of Jack McDonald had taken flesh. Or at least, so it seemed at the time.

When you have been up against the system and suddenly find yourself on a roll of success, you can start disregarding things you normally wouldn't, because you can't see past your own naïve hope that right is finally prevailing. I fell prey to that fault during those heady years, when crimes in the residential schools was still a novel and mostly uncensored topic, and reporters were crawling all over our every word and deed. Until enough kicks to the head have shown us otherwise, we all want to believe that Caesar has reformed himself and will suddenly dispense justice for us.

The first cold gusts of reality began to strike at us even before our IHRAAM Tribunal convened in June, 1998. At a public forum for residential school survivors that we sponsored in April in Port Alberni, some United Church-backed thugs heckled the speakers. One of them – a Tribal Council politician from Port Alberni named Ron Hamilton – went up to Harry Wilson and threatened to kill him if he spoke about the girl's body that he had found at the Alberni school. Harry went mute that day.

"You don't mess with Ron Hamilton" Harry explained to me later.

"He was an enforcer at the Alberni residential school. He used to beat up the other kids and rat them out to the Principal. One word from him and you go missing."

Closer to home, that same week I was confronted outside my east end apartment by someone impersonating a character from a bad cop movie. He was a Mountie, as it turned out.

The spook's name was Gerry Peters. In his capacity as head of the alleged RCMP "investigation" into the Indian residential schools, he had turned up nothing in over three years. Gerry was pretending to imitate a real policeman but failing miserably. He was supposed to fail, after all. Being a flunkey to others didn't seem to sit well with Gerry. Maybe that's why he was pissed off at me that evening.

"We're concerned about all these claims you and Mrs. Nahanee are making about dead children" Gerry said gravely.

"Really? Why is that?" I replied in my best Cheeky Monkey tone.

"Nahanee is not a credible witness" continued Mr. Wannabee Cop.

"Besides, that guy Caldwell who she says killed the girl, he'd never get convicted if he was still alive."

I made a point of blinking twice with a pseudo-dumbfounded expression before replying,

"He wouldn't? How do you know that? I mean, are you the judge and the jury?"

Then Gerry lost it. He sputtered angrily,

"Look, Reverend, some people are getting really upset over what you're doing, and they might try stopping you. For your own good, you'd better come to me before issuing any more press releases about dead Indian children."

I could not resist following up on such a perfect straight line. So naturally, the IHRAAM Tribunal went ahead on schedule, despite Gerry Peters' threat.

The event opened on June 12, 1998 in the Maritime Labour Centre in east Vancouver. IHRAAM paid for the hall and sent three of its officials, Yussuf Kly, Rudy James and his wife Diana, along with ten aboriginal observers from around the continent. The media was out in full force, at least initially.

For several months I had worked overtime to line up nearly thirty residential school survivors to give testimonies to the Tribunal. Over the next three days the observers heard from aging men and women their first-hand accounts of child killings, late night burials, grisly tortures, and medical experiments at six coastal Indian schools. As the witnesses sobbed the names of the killers and those who had helped them, the residential schools matter quickly became more than the restricted "physical and sexual physical abuse" described in the press. These were Crimes against Humanity.

Foremost in that regard were the references people made to deadly medical experiments conducted on themselves and their murdered friends at three state-funded and church-run Indian hospitals in Nanaimo, Duncan and Bella Bella, BC. Sexual sterilizations, drug testing, deliberate virus infection, eye color and mind alteration, and pain threshold testing were described by nine different eyewitnesses. Many of the methods now being deployed against the general population, including deadly viruses and microchip-laced vaccinations, were first tested on children in the Indian hospitals across Canada as early as the 1950's.

Less than a year after our Tribunal and no doubt in response to our publication of these crimes, the Canadian Press began to report that the Catholic, Anglican and United churches routinely allowed native children in their legal care to be used in medical experiments, including food and vitamin deprivation studies.

Despite and perhaps because of these explosive revelations, by the second day of the Tribunal, many of the witnesses grew hesitant to speak. The numbers of people started declining. I learned out why the hard way.

As a hired thug, Dean Wilson was not as subtle as Constable Gerry Peters. At lunch hour on June 13, the burly Indian backed me into a corner and with his big fist around my neck declared,

"Eddie John's pissed off with what you're doing, and he says to stop it if you want to live."

I hadn't the wherewithal at that moment to ask him who the hell Eddie John was. But some of the other Indians blanched later when I mentioned his name.

Helen Michel and Frank Martin knew Ed John very well. As they described in a closed session of the Tribunal, they were both northern Carrier-Sekani Indians who had tangled with him when he was chief of the tribal council there.

"Ed John's the power up north" described Helen.

"He's in with the feds and the big power companies and he runs the cops and judges. All the drug dealing and child trafficking happens through him. Ed has killed people to get their land and traplines. He did it to my cousin. If you criticize him, you get a one-way trip to the lake."

But why is this guy opposed to the Indian residential schools truth coming out? I asked her.

"I told you, he's the government's man. He's signed away our land in treaty talks. He was a goon for the Catholic church at the Lejac residential school. They got him when he was young."

Ed John epitomizes the aboriginal collaborators who became the main obstacle to justice for residential school survivors, and who remain the enemy of most native people in Canada.

These puppets' state-funded cabal known as the Assembly of First Nations consistently opposed any investigation into residential school crimes or to the opening of reported mass graves of children. They consistently silenced their own people who spoke of them. The pale rulers learned long ago to use their brown puppets to manage and wipe out their fellow Indians through the apartheid "Indian Act". I began to see how it all happens, on the ground, as our work progressed.

Despite these attacks, and the disappearance of the media – only *The Globe and Mail* reported that the Tribunal had happened – the event concluded in a positive, nearly euphoric spirit among the IHRAAM officials and observers. They agreed that the evidence they had heard compelled them to recommend to the United Nations that a full-scale investigation be launched in Canada, including at the sites of reported mass graves of children. Such a recommendation was sent by Rudy James and IHRAAM Director Yussuf Kly to UN Human Rights Commissioner Mary Robinson as well as to the UN Secretary-General Kofi Annan.

Neither of them replied, nor did anyone else at the UN. And then the push back began.

One by one, the Tribunal observers dropped away, refusing to add their names to a report of the proceedings that Rudy James and I tried to have published. The IHRAAM Director Yussuf Kly, on his own initiative, reinvented history and disavowed any participation in the Tribunal, despite his actual physical presence there! Kly even contradicted his own press release by claiming that IHRAAM had never sponsored it. Eventually, even Rudy James backed off when smears circulated on the internet about his supposed sexual habits. It all smelled of a professional black-ops campaign.

In fact, the decades-long effort to vilify me and discredit my work really began in the wake of the silencing of the IHRAAM Tribunal. As Amy Tallio, an Alert Bay survivor and one of our sources, said to her sister Irene Starr in August of 1998,

"There's money to be made if you turn against Kevin. Just talk to Jim Craven."

Craven had been one of the Tribunal observers and was the source of the smears against Rudy James.

Craven had earlier been identified and named by the American Indian Movement and Greenpeace as a paid informant for the RCMP and the FBI.

But the source of the shutdown went much higher, as I learned over the years that followed. It came from the office of the Prime Minister of Canada, Jean Chretien.

According to a former operative of the Canadian Security Intelligence Service (CSIS) named Grant Wakefield, on April 3, 1998, a cabinet directive of the Prime Minister's Office (PMO) ordered "E" Division of the RCMP in B.C. to monitor, infiltrate and conduct covert operations to destroy any groups that independently investigated crimes at Indian residential schools or hospitals. This secret Directive was implemented and led by RCMP Staff Sergeant Peter Montague just prior to the IHRAAM Tribunal and was clearly aimed at it.

As Wakefield described to me in two conversations I had with him in the spring of 2006, the Chretien directive was an explicit state terror campaign that accounted for the smears, disruptions and attacks that began against our efforts and me during this time, and that continue today.

The purpose of these black ops was to wipe out any alternative narrative of the residential school genocide that conflicted with the "official", benign version being crafted at that time by Church and State; namely, that a few "bad decisions", and not genocide, took place in the residential schools.

The outcome of the Chretien Directive was the death of at least seven aboriginal members of our movement in Vancouver and Winnipeg: Harriett Nahanee, Johnny "Bingo" Dawson, Ricky Lavallee, Harry Wilson, William Combes, Edna Phillips and Ron Barbour. All these friends died of clear foul play in the period following the Tribunal after they had publicly confronted the Catholic, Anglican and United churches for their crimes.

But there were even bigger things at stake for the government and its church allies. The Chretien Directive prevented any serious effort to prosecute these perpetrators for genocide and the deaths of countless children. But it also concealed the fact that the killing and disappearance of aboriginal people was continuing, and at the hands of the same people who had caused the residential school atrocities.

For example, the black-ops teams that disrupted and buried the IHRAAM Tribunal under the direction of RCMP officer Peter Montague performed a similar attack on the grassroots efforts to expose the growing numbers of missing native women across B.C. Since I played a key role in both movements, I became a primary target of these black-ops efforts that have spanned more than two decades.

In the words of Peter Montague, spoken to Grant Wakefield on August 12, 1998,

"Take down Annett and you take down the issue."

Nevertheless, the thrones of the guilty were being shaken by the ones who had not been expected to survive. It was now a simple matter of who would break first.

…………………….

Another life beckoned to me at that same time. My application to a doctoral program at Cambridge University had been accepted. I was suddenly presented with a fork in my road: a way out of the uncertainty and betrayal of the past years. But it would mean abandoning our burgeoning cause and my own children for several years.

As I struggled with the choice during my forty third year, the prescient words of my murdered friend Fidel from Chiapas came back to me: *"Whenever I was tempted to flee, I went to the poorest child in the camp and realized that she couldn't escape. So why should I?"*

In truth, I was as rooted in the soil that held the dead children as I was in the lives of my daughters, who at ages nine and six were in the clutch of an abusive mother. Leaving them was not an option for me, even as I knew the consequence of staying in the line of fire. It was a fate I accepted as readily as William Wordsworth's "happy warrior". *

....

* Who comprehends his trust, and to the same keeps faithful with a singleness of aim; And therefore, does not stoop, nor lie in wait for wealth, or honours, or for worldly state; But who, if he be called upon to face some awful moment to which Heaven has joined great issues, good or bad for humankind, is happy as a Lover; and attired with sudden brightness, like a Man inspired; Or if he must fall, to sleep without his fame, and leave a dead unprofitable name, Finds comfort in himself and in his cause; And, while the mortal mist is gathering, draws his breath in confidence of Heaven's applause: This is the happy Warrior; this is he that every man in arms should wish to be.

Besides, what sane man would want to vanish from the scene now that the action was just beginning? Every day the guilty parties kept stumbling over themselves as they comically donned an ill-fitting garb of politically correct self-righteousness.

Within a few months of our IHRAAM Tribunal, the feds announced what some bright boy in Ottawa had named the "Aboriginal Healing Fund", which was aimed at only certain Indian residential school survivors. This slimy effort was known in native circles as the "Aboriginal Hush Fund", since a gag order accompanied the pittances doled out to the chosen few who received it. My name for it was the "Caucasian Healing Fund", considering how its aim and consequence was to mend not Indians but white peoples' guilt and legal liability.

The new millennium in Canada arrived in that sort of vein of tragedy and farce. Even as the national press reported new discoveries (made mostly by our small movement) of the church-run medical experiments where native kids were deliberately starved or sterilized, the perpetrators spoke of "healing" the slaughter with enough bucks and blarney.

At the same time, the same churches were publicly bemoaning their supposed financial bankruptcies more than they were the legions of children who they had tortured, eviscerated, and slaughtered.

The time had come to up the ante on the entire mess. So, one spring day in the year 2000, I called a meeting in Vancouver and twenty people formed a permanent Truth Commission into Genocide in Canada that would continue the work of the sabotaged IHRAAM Tribunal. Soon after that, I authored the first book ever written on our home-grown genocide, entitled *"Hidden from History: The Canadian Holocaust."* All the research, documents, and testimonies I had gathered for five years that would have ensured me a lucrative academic career became instead a bullet fired by the lost and the forgotten.

My job was to make sure that it was aimed well.

....

CTV News Vancouver, Monday, May 6, 2002
(*This interview was never broadcast*)

Interviewer: Can you tell us your name and what you're doing here today?

Indian: It's Val Nahanee. I'm here supporting my mother Harriet, that's her over there.

Interviewer: Do you know why she's protesting?

Indian: Of course I do! I was right next to her when that United Church guy threatened to kill her!

Interviewer: He claims that it was your mother who threatened him first.

Indian: Yeah, and he also says nobody ever died in one of their stinking residential schools. You gonna believe him? My mom saw that bastard Caldwell kill a little girl at the Alberni school!

Interviewer: What were you doing in Port Alberni, Val?

Indian: We were looking for the graves of all the kids they killed in that residential school. There's lots of bodies out back behind the water pipeline.

Interviewer: *And if you found those alleged graves, then what?*

Indian: We'd bring those children home. They need a proper burial. Then we'd find out who did it.

Interviewer: *Are you part of the Truth Commission, Val?*

Indian: I sure am. You should read this book, it tells the real story.

(She hands the reporter a copy of "Hidden from History: The Canadian Holocaust". He refuses to accept it)

Interviewer: *Do you really want to see the churches taken to court and charged with murder?*

Indian: Well, don't you think it was murder?

Interviewer: *That's not my place to say ...*

Indian: What would you want if they killed your children?

The interviewer signals to turn off the camera and walks away from Val Nahanee.

………………..

In learning how to battle the Goliath of Church and State over a few decades, I have had to acquire the long view.

Normally we measure actions and results in terms of weeks, not years: especially as political activists. Public campaigns are deemed a failure if they don't cause Caesar to concede something after a round of obligatory and ritualized protest. But in the case of our Truth Commission, we were challenging the very foundations of Canada: its self-image and false history, its legislated apartheid, and its vested interests of land grabs and foreign rule. All these things rest on an enormous legacy of genocide that is denied at every level because of the simple fact that it is continuing.

In the short-term view, our efforts seemed to fail. Every time we raised an issue or unearthed a new crime, the government would wait a month and then embrace it while spinning and coating it to make themselves look good.

By 2003, the government had quickly stepped in to cover the costs and legal fallout for the churches that were responsible for the crime, while making noises of launching "healing and reconciliation" programs for the residential school survivors: a refrain echoed by every bought and paid for tribal chief across the country. To the blithely uninformed it looked as if Canada was finally "doing the right thing by its Indians", to quote the government-parroting CBC.

But all that was illusion. The long view shows how desperate those official measures were. For anyone who still remembered our Tribunal and the public movement it engendered, it was obvious that the perpetrators of genocide in Canada were following the lead and the issues defined by us, especially after foreign indigenous groups like the Mayans began publicly criticizing Canada at the United Nations in the wake of our Tribunal.

Following Sun Tzu in his *Art of War*, our battle had been won by us before it was fought because our smaller force had defined and shaped the field of conflict and then held our ground. We defined the issue as that of genocide, not "abuse", and eventually the entire nation agreed with us and adopted our language, against its will and every vested interest.

This initial victory was the consequence of my year-in and year-out tenacity. My persistence had sustained our movement and forced it to dig ever more deeply into the crimes in our midst and confront them ever more strongly. Over the next few years, that determination began to reap even greater results. I often received proof of this in unexpected ways.

Whispers Wind was one such surprise. A small, aged Ojibway elder from Winnipeg who went by the name Louis Daniels, he met me at a healing circle there in the first year of the new millennium. By the end of the day he had adopted me into his Crane clan and given me the name that I still carry proudly: Gano GeeKeeway GeeKeedoh - Eagle Strong Voice.

"Wear the name proudly, Kevin, because you are doing a job I can't do and that's to speak loudly to your people of their wrongs and warn them of the evil that is to come" Louis told me.

When he was a young boy in 1947, he journeyed in a vision from his imprisonment in the Brandon Indian residential school to a secret governmental meeting in Ottawa. He later recognized Prime Minister Louis St. Laurent and other politicians at the gathering.

"They were talking about how to wipe out all the Ojibways in ten years" Louis explained.

"It was a whole plan they had using doctors, drugs and soldiers. I knew the Grandfathers brought me there to be a witness so I could warn my people. I've spent my life doing that just like you're doing."

Louis was one of a few lingering traditional elders and witnesses to genocide who reached out to me the more publicly vocal I became. Fortunately, by then we had compensated for the waning interest by the corporate media in our work with our own public radio program.

Our weekly show began broadcasting in the spring of 2001 over the airwaves of Vancouver Co-op Radio, located in the Downtown Eastside. We called the program "Hidden from History", and it quickly became a broad platform for eyewitnesses to the Canadian genocide. Our movement had secured its own public voice that helped swell our influence.

Until it was shut down by the government in 2010, our show gave voice to many residential school survivors who were living on the streets and who often wandered into the studio to tell of their tortures. *Hidden from History* helped to spark and build our grassroots movement even more.

Occupying churches also helped the process. Over the next decade, it got to be a habit with me and a few unbought and unbossed Indians like Louis Daniels and many anonymous street Indians in Vancouver. But the practice of "hitting the pews", as we called it, began quite spontaneously.

On April 15, 2005, our movement held the first Annual Aboriginal Holocaust Remembrance Day and set up a group to continue the event called The Friends and Relatives of the Disappeared (FRD).

A bunch of us gathered in the rain that day outside Holy Rosary Catholic Cathedral in downtown Vancouver with our new banner declaring *"All the Children Need a Proper Burial"*. After leafletting sullen mass-goers with little effect, somebody suggested we go into the church to get out of the rain and dry off. So, in we trooped.

The church ushers were too outnumbered to stop our advance, and before long we were clustered all over the sanctuary. The head priest, who wore the biggest frown, barked orders at us to clear out. His name was Glen Dion, and soon after that he was accused by his own church staff of stealing over $65,000 from the parish funds, which perhaps explained his touchiness.

The other cleric was a smoother operator. With a plastic grimace on his face, the priest announced to the confused worshippers,

"It seems we have some new friends with us today. Perhaps they'd like to take a seat and join us in our worship service."

Harriett Nahanee stepped out from our group and snapped back at him,

"We aren't your friends and we sure as hell won't sit in your devil worshipping church! Not until you give us back the children you killed!"

There was no stopping Harriett once she was on a roll, and without another word she made a beeline for the pulpit. She solemnly ascended the steps and spoke to the parishioners about the crimes of their church against her people, and of how their own God called to them to do justice to those they had wronged.

Neither the numbed parishioners nor the priests knew what to do. We took good advantage of their shock. By the time the police arrived, we had scattered our leaflets to the crowd and left in a dignified procession. But the real victory was that as we left the church and despite the altercation, the entire congregation rose in silent respect. The priests stared helplessly. In the very bowels of the enemy we had won the high ground and perhaps some of their hearts and minds as well.

That was a good day. And the group of us saw no reason not to repeat the performance and count even greater coups against our enemy.

After that incident, something shifted. All the downtown Vancouver churches were gripped in a comical fear and stayed alert for any sign of me or any Indians approaching their worship services. My picture was posted in the offices of these churches with frenzied instructions to contact the police if I appeared near their churches.

Naturally, we used that hysteria to our advantage. Sometimes we would announce we were hitting Holy Rosary and show up instead at the nearby Anglican or United churches. If we didn't occupy the church *en masse* we'd split up and infiltrate the service one by one, talking to and leafletting the people in the pews. With the advantage of a small, mobile, and unpredictable guerrilla force, we kept our adversary in a continual state of uncertainty and defensiveness.

As Sun Tzu advises, our actions provoked our enemy into ever-increasing acts of self destruction.

For in response, the churches hired private security guards who started monitoring everyone coming into church on Sundays. They even began frisking people. The parishioners were outraged, and their usual decorum collapsed. It was all a psychological war and we held the advantage. The churches were guilty of monstrous crimes, and they could see that judgement was approaching them in the form of aboriginal people holding a banner.

Our direct actions grew with what they fed on. With each new confrontation, the media made our little group seem like an army, raising the paranoia level among the church officials. The truth was that we were indeed much more than our numbers. For we represented every victim of religious carnage over two thousand years.

After our first actions, the Vancouver police began absurdly following me around the Downtown East Side, especially on Sunday mornings. In this way I was used as a decoy to distract the cops while our group hit a new, unsuspecting church. In truth, all of us "church whackers" were having fun: one of the requirements of any successful direct action, according to the venerable radical Saul Alinsky.

In his book *Rules for Radicals*, Alinsky advises us to remember that power is not only what we have but what our enemy thinks we have. We experienced that truth in spades. The media blackout on me and our campaign had not started by then, and our actual impact and numbers were inflated by the usual sensationalism of the press. That helped us to count coup against the churches on occasion and eventually forced the government to step in.

Our crowning victory happened during 2007 and early 2008, when our adversaries finally broke. The signs of their collapse were everywhere by then.

Our escalating occupations of his Holy Rosary Cathedral had made Catholic Archbishop Raymond Roussin suffer a nervous breakdown and resign from his office. *Yes! Indians One, Child Killers Nothing!* But the lawyers for all three of the guilty churches exhibited the same kind of desperate defeatism. The lot of them began besieging me with letters and phone calls demanding to know what was required of them for us to stop disrupting their church services.

By that time, our protests and Sunday seizures had spread to other cities. One Sunday early in 2007, a Mohawk clan mother occupied the ornate pulpit of Metropolitan United Church in Toronto and evicted that church from her traditional territory. The same expulsion order was posted on the Anglican and Catholic churches as the TV cameras whirred. The Pharisees were more than a little upset. And our momentum continued to build.

With perfect timing, we launched into this firestorm at that moment what proved to be the *coup de grace* against the killers: a documentary film we had produced called *Unrepentant.* The film told the unvarnished story of the Indian residential school massacre, featuring many of its survivors. Within a month of its release in January of 2007, it had won two film awards and received nearly half a million hits on youtube.

The film swept like a brushfire through the minds and communities of natives. It was even viewed in the corridors of power. In the words of former Member of Parliament Gary Merasty,

"After Unrepentant, we all had to sit up and take notice."

Merasty was a Cree Indian from Saskatchewan who briefly played a key role in forcing a change. After watching *Unrepentant*, he stood up in Parliament in March of 2007 and asked Indian Affairs Minister Jim Prentice when the dead Indian residential school children would be given a proper burial. The next day, Prentice promised an "inquiry" into the missing children that never happened. But he also announced a "Truth and Reconciliation Commission" (TRC) into Indian residential schools.

Although the TRC became a huge coverup and obstruction of justice, and would not convene for another year, the Pandora's Box had been officially opened. Our movement was determined that it would not be closed.

That formal acknowledgement of what we had been unearthing and claiming for many years gave others the green light, too. On April 24, 2007 and for the first time, Canada's leading newspaper, *The Globe and Mail*, agreed with us by declaring that half the children had died in the residential schools.

Its front-page article was entitled *"Natives died in droves as Ottawa ignored warnings"*. Suddenly it became permitted and even fashionable to speak about dead Indian children. That opening gave new legitimacy to our campaign and more openings and levers.

It was not a bad way for me to enter my fifties.

As the word of our victory spread, total strangers would run up and embrace me, or happily flash me a thumbs up sign from their passing vehicles. The mudslingers and internet smears diminished. Most important, our people and many survivors began to feel hopeful. New voices began to speak out and more names were named.

The greatest gift for me at that time was to witness the miracle of change bubble up in once-ruined lives. One night at the Hobbema Cree reservation south of Edmonton, I stood among a hundred native people and many survivors who had just struggled and sobbed their way through our film *Unrepentant*. A young Cree woman got up angrily and declared,

"I've spent my whole life hating my parents for being so messed up and for messing me up, but now I don't have to hate them anymore. I see it wasn't their fault. Now I can put my hate where it belongs. The whites were trying to wipe us out. There's a word for that: genocide. Now we can see how and why it happened here. But what I don't get is why it took a white man to tell us this? Why didn't our own people tell us?"

An even more soul-searching question now faced my own people:

Who are we to have done the crime in the first place? And would we take responsibility for it in anything but a self-serving way?

I received the answer in full force over the years that followed. For even at the height of our success in halting Goliath, our adversaries were preparing to wipe out the memory of the crime and of those of us who had raised it up for the world to see.

Chapter Seven: Cover-Ups, Court Trials and the Collapse of a Pope

The Truth and Reconciliation Commission ... shall not hold formal hearings, nor act as a public inquiry, nor conduct a legal process; it shall not possess subpoena powers nor have the power to compel attendance at its events; it shall not take down as evidence any reference to a capital crime or to the alleged criminal complicity of any group or individual; it shall not name names of those accused of wrongdoing and shall require closed sessions if such names are mentioned; it shall come to no conclusion regarding the liability or culpability of any group or individual in wrongdoing ...
- from *Mandate of The Truth and Reconciliation Commission*, Section Two, Ottawa, 2008

The purpose and mandate of the ITCCS is a) to document, publicize, prosecute, and punish individuals and institutions, including corporations, churches and government, for crimes against children, and b) to stop these criminal persons and bodies from operating.
– from The Founding Proclamation Establishing the International Tribunal of Crimes of Church and State (ITCCS), Dublin, June 15, 2010

I confirm that the remains I examined in your presence are those of a small child, being a socket bone from a

very young female. This bone has been burned and cut.
I confirm that this bone was recovered from a site
adjacent to the former Anglican Church's Mohawk Indian
Residential School in Brantford, Ontario. Based on this
find, I will recommend that the Ontario government
immediately issue a Coroner's Warrant and conduct a
thorough forensic examination of the graves that the
Mohawk elders have unearthed at this site.
– from a written statement to the author from Greg
Olson, Provincial Coroner's Office of Ontario, January 9,
2012

In the Matter of The People v. Joseph Ratzinger,
Elizabeth Windsor et al, the unanimous verdict of the
Jury is that the accused persons, their agents and their
Bodies Corporate are guilty as charged under the two
indictments of the Court, namely, for committing crimes
against humanity and concealing those crimes. The
sentence of the Jury is that the guilty persons are
sentenced in absentia to life imprisonment without the
possibility of parole and that their authority, assets and
properties and those of their respective Bodies
Corporate are hereby and forever forfeited and rendered
null and void.
– from _The Proceedings of Case Docket No. 02252013-_
01, The People v. Ratzinger, Windsor et al in The
International Common Law Court of Justice, Criminal
Trial Division, Brussels, February 25, 2013

Wilf Price was a Haida native who had endured the usual gamut of residential school tortures as a boy. After years at my side, he suddenly dropped out of our group at the height of our protests during the spring of 2007. So, I was surprised when shortly afterwards he sent me an urgent request to meet him at our usual spot in the Ovaltine Café.

"I didn't think you'd see me" the large man said into his coffee. "I know I fucked up again."

"Forget it, Wilf" I said, wondering if I sounded reassuring. The Indian continued,

"I lose my nerve a lot more these days, all those fucking memories keep coming back."

Wilf stared for awhile at the people trudging along Hastings street. His expression was the same as when he had described to me the electrodes that Brother Murphy had attached to his penis and ears at the Lejac residential school when he was six years old.

I was about to say something when Wilf gave a deep shudder and muttered,

"I don't want to see all of you get hurt, Kev. You don't know what you're going up against".

Coming when it did, his remark didn't make sense to me. We were on a roll, and the government was buckling. We had fought for a dozen years against incredible odds and had begun to move mountains. Wasn't it a time for celebrating?

Wilf could read my thoughts.

"Look Kev, they're saying what we want to hear right now to take the pressure off themselves and buy the time to shut it all down. Just you watch."

Despite my reticence at his words, I took them seriously, for Wilf knew what he was talking about.

For some years he had been a west coast delegate to the puppet government body known as the "Assembly of First Nations" (AFN) until he couldn't stomach their corruption anymore. But he still had contacts on the inside, and according to Wilf they were all saying the same thing now about the residential school issue: Get ready for the Big Spin and Shutdown.

"These guys buy who they can and kill the ones they can't buy" Wild said somberly.

"I've seen them do it on a dozen different reserves to their opposition. The feds and the chiefs, they're not going to let what you're doing survive."

Over the following years, Wilf's grim prophecy bore itself out, as our people were killed off or scared off while the media fogged the genocidal reality of the residential schools. Despite its initial lip service to the issue, the government made no effort to investigate the missing children or establish a "Truth and Reconciliation Commission". The entire topic was deftly avoided in Parliament and in the media as if it had never been raised. Gary Merasty resigned as a Member of Parliament and was hired by Cameco Uranium company in Saskatchewan, a firm tied closely to the government. Jim Prentice was shuffled out of his spot as Indian Affairs Minister into a lesser portfolio. Even sympathetic journalists who had tried digging deeper into the national genocide found themselves canned or muzzled.

Nevertheless, this rapid housecleaning did not quell the outcry we had raised. The genie was out of the bottle. Traditional elders not tied to the AFN began calling for digs of suspected graves at former residential schools, especially after I published a list of twenty-eight mass grave sites of children. More protests erupted outside and inside Catholic, Anglican, and United churches across the country. At reservations in Manitoba and Ontario, local Ojibway natives evicted Catholic priests and seized their church buildings. Osoyoos Indians in central BC chased the priest out of his church at gunpoint.

At this time, during 2007 and 2008, our group known as Friends and Relatives of the Disappeared (FRD) reached the peak of its impact, using new methods to pressure the guilty. We expanded our sit-ins at government offices in Vancouver, Winnipeg and Toronto, where we vowed *"an escalating campaign of civil disobedience to force the government and churches to return the remains of the more than 50,000 children they claimed died in the schools"*. ("Native group threatens trouble", <u>24 Hour News</u>, May 24, 2007).

Further, in February of 2008, our FRD announced that it was *"preparing to take the federal government to international criminal court and disinter the bodies of native children. 'We need a genuine war crimes court with the power to subpoena and prosecute the churches and Canadian government' said Kevin Annett, a group spokesperson."* ("Native group warns of international court action", <u>The National Post</u>, February 13, 2008).

As it turned out, the evasion and stalling tactics by the government were the result of a major crisis that had arisen between them and their partners in crime, the Catholic, Anglican, and United churches.

The churches relied on Ottawa to continue shielding them from the consequences of their wrongs, as they had for over a century. At first the feds had done so, taking the heat for the residential schools, picking up the churches' legal bills and enacting legislation to limit and restrict the personal injury lawsuits brought by survivors. But with the growing public exposure of the deaths of children and the genocidal nature of the schools, Ottawa suddenly had more to consider than just placating the churches.

Quite simply, the world, and international law, was suddenly watching Canada. As the main party to the crime, the churches had the most to lose from such exposure. They felt their traditional control of the issue slipping and they began panicking.

As a result, after the government spoke publicly of investigating missing children early in 2007, the churches pressured Ottawa to stall the launching of a "Truth and Reconciliation Commission" for a year to allow them time to destroy their incriminating records and grave sites with the help of the RCMP. The destruction of these crime scenes and evidence was sanctioned by the government and courts. The TRC was then established as a toothless body by the churches and government themselves so that they would never face exposure or prosecution.

As part of this grotesque obstruction of justice, the serial killer of Church and State legally indemnified itself from the residential schoosl fallout through special Order in Council legislation, outside the purview of Parliament or the public. In effect these institutions absolved themselves of their crime and appointed themselves as their own judge and jury.

The entire, massive coverup employed the new code word for genocide in Canada popularly known as "healing and reconciliation".

The culmination of this huge damage control effort occurred in Parliament on July 8, 2008, when the Harper government issued a public "apology" for the Indian residential schools. But it did so not as a statement of regret, responsibility, or liability, or while Parliament sat in session, stripping the statement of any legal or political significance. As with the subsequent TRC fiasco that continued for seven years and never uncovered the grave of a single child, the "apology" was nothing more than a slick public relations gesture that changed nothing.

Many people saw this gimmick for what it was, especially in the native world. When the televised apology was broadcast at the Carnegie Center in downtown Vancouver, I watched as most of the Indians present either got up and left in anger or guffawed and catcalled the proceedings. And yet "official" Canadian society endorsed and applauded the fraud and kept itself blind to the Emperor's nakedness.

The lackey AFN "chiefs" were even worse. They sat dutifully alongside Prime Minister Harper when he read the bland, lawyer-crafted apology that never mentioned a dead child. And not a single media outlet or politician dared to ask how the parties to a crime could investigate themselves or pose as the "healers" of their own victims.

The Big Fix was in. And so naturally what followed was its twin evil sister, the Big Erasure.

Over the next few years, the memory of what our grassroots movement had brought to light was wiped from the public mind and memory, including the alternative narrative that showed how our homegrown genocide was continuing. I began to encounter that erasure immediately. After being routinely quoted and interviewed, I was suddenly censored from the Canadian media. As with a banned person in apartheid-era South Africa, my name was scrubbed out of any public discourse and I was no longer mentioned in press reports. I was now officially known by the pejorative title of "a controversial ex-minister".

Similarly, none of the growing protests around the country or the hard evidence provided by witnesses were reported any longer by the muzzled national media, even as churches continued to be occupied and graves were unearthed.

An official Night and Fog had been placed over the Canadian Holocaust, and over me.

....

A tornado of unusual intensity struck the center of Rome this morning. It was the first such disturbance in over forty years.
– *Il Manifesto,* Rome, October 12, 2009

It was revealed today that Pope Benedict recently issued a confidential memo to his Bishops ordering them to destroy any evidence of child rape in the Catholic church and to silence all those involved. The Pope made it clear that police authorities were not to be told of incidents of child abuse in his church, and that anyone reporting them were to be punished.
– *SF1 Switzerland* TV news report, October 14, 2009

A Canadian clergyman has described the abuse experienced by native children in residential schools in Canada as identical to abuse in Ireland. "The stories are identical including the extent to which police and government colluded to protect the perpetrators" said the Rev. Kevin Annett, a former minister of the United Church of Canada. Mr. Annett spoke at a demonstration outside the Dail yesterday ... He said there was a need to "unite across borders to let people know they're not alone". He had protested outside the Vatican in Rome and said Pope Benedict was "criminally complicit" in abuse because of the policy not to inform police when cases were reported.

- from "Abuse in Canadian residential schools identical to here, says clergyman" in *The Irish Times*, Dublin, April 15, 2010

The September morning in 2009 had been a typically rainy one at my home in Nanaimo when the call came that caused sunlight to appear. It was from Genoa, Italy.

The caller was Marina Dondero, the Vice-President of the Province of Liguria that rings the city. She invited me to come and address her cabinet and the Italian people about the genocide of Indians in my country.

"It is what we owe to them" she explained through an interpreter.

"Christopher Columbus came from our city. The genocide in your country began here."

The past year had seen our campaign in Canada sag as the government's spin and containment operation unfolded. Many people in our movement had dropped away, either in despair at seeing new official lies prevail, or out of a naïve belief that the perpetrators had "come around" and there was nothing left for us to do. The press ignored us completely by then and the invitations to me to speak at campuses and on alternative media had plummeted. Marina Dondero's invitation changed all that, in ways I could not have imagined.

For years I had envisioned myself standing outside the Vatican in the company of many spirits and confronting the source of the evil with more than words. Now I had my opportunity. The trip to Genoa was a stage setting for the main event at St. Peter's square in Rome.

The sky was overcast that morning when I stood in the square. Before me loomed the grey edifice of the Vatican, perched appropriately enough on the former palace grounds of the psychopathic Roman Emperor Caligula. In truth, it felt like I was facing a great nothingness.

In my hands that day I held the soil from graves of children who had died in Catholic Indian schools in Canada. I was there to honor their memory in the face of the thing that had killed them. But quickly the memorial became a public exorcism. It was October 11, 2009.

I can't remember all of the words I spoke that morning, or how the normally vigilant Vatican and Rome police walked past me without seeming to notice, when normally any protest or "unapproved" ceremony there is prohibited and immediately stopped. My words spoke to the dark governing entity of Church of Rome and commanded that it reveal itself and depart. I invoked the spirit of all those who had been violated and killed by it over two thousand years, and I felt those souls standing with me. And together, something epic acted through us.

The proof of our impact came the next morning when a tornado struck the center of Rome for the first time in more than forty years. Just two days later, the first media reports surfaced that linked then-Pope Benedict, Joseph Ratzinger, to the coverup of child trafficking networks in his church. The entity had begun to reveal itself, as during the first stage of any exorcism.

People seemed shocked when Joseph Ratzinger resigned from his office in February 2013. But his collapse was the outcome of the whirlwind that I had helped unleash against the world's oldest and richest criminal syndicate.

Word of my action spread quickly among survivors of church crimes in Europe, and a group of them in Ireland invited me to meet with them in the spring of 2010. At that meeting was sown the seed that would become the International Tribunal of Crimes of Church and State (ITCCS): the first citizen-led international body ever to prosecute and convict child killing institutions, and to force a Pope to resign from his office.

....

Rosaleen Rogers looked like she hadn't slept in a week, which is not unusual for a survivor of childhood torture. We stood together that day in a protest with fifty other people outside the Irish Parliament in Dublin.

Masking her bone-weariness with classic Emerald Isle gallows humor, Rosaleen remarked that if I hung around her long enough, I might end up with electrodes clamped to the more sensitive parts of my body. During the Troubles, she had lost a brother to savage police beatings in prison. Torture was not a new thing in her family.

Rosaleen spoke plainly and powerfully that day when she spoke through a loudspeaker to fifty other people who rallied outside the Dail Erin.

"The Catholic church locked me up as a teenager in Clonmel Mental Hospital" she said haltingly.

"They did experiments on me in there and starved me nearly to death. At one point I was down to fifty-five pounds. I haven't been able to keep food down for forty years and I've been unable to work. It ruined my life. I've lost everything."

Rosaleen stared at the angry faces around her and then said firmly,

"I'm not here to complain to anyone. I've tried that. The Archbishop has no heart or soul in him. We need to get justice for ourselves. I want a Tribunal to establish what happened to me and all the others who didn't survive. I want to know who harmed me. They all belong in jail."

Those of us who were with Rosaleen that day took her call to heart. As veterans of many battles, we had passed the stage of mere reaction, and of the dead-end approach of begging for crumbs from the ones that harmed us. We chose to end the sickness once and for all by uprooting its cause. And so that same week we gathered in a community center in the north end of Dublin and formed the ITCCS.

The purpose of our Tribunal was simple: to form an international body to expose, prosecute and stop any institution of Church and State that harms children, including by disestablishing it. Our aim was a typically Irish way of thinking.

"You lock up one priest for raping a kid and five others do the same" yelled another woman at our meeting, a firebrand named Mary Kelly who I came to know well.

"The fuckers get away with it 'cause they're all protected by the law and the pope himself. You've got to get rid of their power, their tax exemptions, and all their privileges. Seize their property and dump the whole goddamned church is what I say! They've lost their right to exist!"

A radical approach to some, Mary's words and our mandate are basic common sense to anyone who has ever gone up against institutionalized crime. Combined with our call to link hands across borders with all the other victims of Church and State, the ITCCS was from its inception something new in the world. We were citizens who through our own natural sovereignty were putting the entire system on trial.

The word went out quickly, and by the end of that summer six different groups of church survivors in England, America and Italy had contacted us and affiliated with our Tribunal.

With the assistance of a Spanish judge named Baltazar Garzon and other legal advisers, our new group began preparing an International Common Law Court of Justice that would put the Vatican and its affiliates on trial. And in Ireland, England, Italy, Holland, Belgium, France and America, our allies began picketing and occupying Catholic churches, inspired by our successful example in Canada.

This cross-fertilization worked in both directions across the Atlantic, sustaining our movement and aiding me to maneuver around my blacklisting and the Canadian media ban I faced. And so, after the ITCCS began making headlines in Europe during 2011, a group of native elders of the Grand River Mohawks in Ontario heard about us and sent me an invitation. They wanted to have the remains of their murdered relatives brought home from the grounds of the former Anglican Indian residential school in Brantford: the infamous Mohawk Institute, known to survivors as the "Mush Hole".

I was about to raise the temperature again in my own country.

....

Mohawk researchers, with the aid of former United Church minister Kevin Annett, have unearthed what they believe is at least one human bone fragment: that of a small child of around four or five years old ... The find was made while conducting a preliminary test dig of an area of the former Mohawk Institute in Brantford.
– from "Possible child's remains uncovered at Mush Hole" by Jim Windle in *Tekawennake, Six Nations and Mississaugas*, November 30, 2011, Vol. 48, No. 17.

It was appropriate that the year in which so much death was revealed would begin with the killing of one of our dearest and best people. He was a diminutive and soft-spoken Salish Indian named William Combes.

I first met William early in 2006 when he spoke on my *Hidden from History* radio program of atrocities he had witnessed as a boy in the Kamloops and Mission Catholic Indian schools. William became a fixture of our movement after that, always present at our protests and occupations despite how he became physically ill at the sight of a cross.

"They used to wave it in my face whenever they were shoving that cattle prod up my ass" he explained laconically.

Neither William's childhood trauma nor his own alcoholic disability deterred or defeated him. What finally slew him was his knowledge of an incident involving someone named Elizabeth Windsor.

William was eleven years old when it happened, on the afternoon of October 10, 1964. The scene was the Catholic Kamloops Indian residential school in central British Columbia.

"The priests told us kids that the Queen was going to visit us, so all of us got bathed and were given good clothes. She and Prince Phillip showed up all by themselves, no TV cameras or flunkies. We all went to Dead Man's Creek for a picnic. They gave us Kool-Aid that made us pass out. But I saw the Queen leave with some of the local kids, seven boys and three girls. They all vanished. Nobody ever saw any of those children again."

William always hesitated to talk about the incident in public, but in February of 2011, a chance opened for his words to have some impact. A Swiss TV station wanted to interview him about what he had seen, and the ITCCS invited William to speak to a human rights panel in London, England.

William was happier and more confident in those final days, partly because he had stopped drinking alcohol in the wake of our successful occupation of a Catholic cathedral. He readily agreed to go to Europe, and I made all the travel arrangements.

Three days before his scheduled departure, William was forcibly detained by three RCMP officers at the Vancouver Native Health Centre and taken to St. Paul's Catholic hospital in Vancouver. After forty-eight hours he died, on February 26, 2011.

According to Chloe Kirker, his attending nurse,

"Billy Combes didn't die of tubercular meningitis like the coroner claims. He had no symptoms of TB. He was infected with something. I found lumbar punctures on him where he had been injected, but they didn't have him on an I.V. at all. I objected to that but was ignored by the doctor and head nurse. Billy's symptoms pointed to arsenic poisoning. He was weak, sore, dizzy and had what are called Mees Lines on his fingernails. By denying him an I.V., the arsenic was concentrated in his body and the deadly effects were made more rapid. It was obvious that somebody wanted him dead."

William Combes was one of seven native members of our campaign to die of foul play during this time.

The summons from the Grand River Mohawks in Brantford came to me soon after William had been killed. Nine elders from the Turtle and Wolf clans signed a letter inviting me to their territory to help search for the remains of children who had died at the Anglican residential school called the Mush Hole:

"We the Mohawks of the Grand River territory desire to have forensic investigations conducted on the grounds of the former Mohawk Institute … We want to know where the children who died are buried and how they died and to have them disinterred and brought home for a proper burial according to our customs …We authorize Kevin Annett Eagle Strong Voice to work on this project. We grant him our full support and protection and ask that he take the evidence of these crimes to the ITCCS hearings next September in London, England. We support and fully endorse the ITCCS and we call on all residential school survivors to do the same."

These nine signatories were traditional elders who stood outside the state-run "Chief and Council" known as the Six Nations Confederacy. But even the government chiefs were feeling the pressure to investigate the Mush Hole mass graves, which witnesses had already identified during public meetings in Brantford. All of them knew about me and the ITCCS.

"You're the one who has to force this out into the open, Kevin" I was told by Bill Squire, one of the nine elders, the day I first met them in the Kanata Center just a hundred yards from the Mush Hole.

"We're all fighting each other. We need an outsider to make us take the next step of digging up the proof and bringing those children home. There's a lot of fear among our people about what'll happen if we do that, but it's got to be done."

I was indeed walking into a hornet's nest. The Mohawks had traditionally resisted colonialism and recently led land reclamations against the RCMP. But many of them as children had suffered tortures beyond belief in the Mush Hole, and they quailed at the thought of re-opening that house of horrors.

That fear divided and factionalized their nation on the issue.

Fortunately, many of the younger Mohawks didn't harbor such fears. They wanted the dig to happen. Sparked by the nine elders, they soon stepped forward as The Men's Fire Group to provide security at our meetings and our surveys and excavations.

In hindsight, it's amazing that we were able to get as far as we did. Our plans were openly discussed at community meetings to which anyone was invited, especially eyewitnesses who could identify grave sites. One of them, a former student named Geronimo Henry, had helped to bury other children in a grove fifty feet from the Mush Hole buildings.

"You see all that piled up earth?" he said when we first paced the grounds, pointing next to the school building.

"That wasn't there before. You dig there and you'll find bodies. That's where we buried them at night."

Lots of people knew about the Mush Hole graves. Tara Froman, the curator of the nearby Woodland Cultural Center, told me soon after I arrived,

"When the Center was built in 1982, they had to halt construction because they found a lot of little skeletons. The OPP *(Ontario Provincial Police)* roped off the area and took the bones away. They wouldn't say where they took them, but I learned some bones were destroyed and others stored at the Royal Ontario Museum."

Built in 1832 by the British Crown and the Church of England, the Mohawk Institute was the first and the longest-operating Indian residential school in Canada, closing in 1979. The building itself is ominous. All over its worn bricks is scribbled the graffiti of long-past children, declaring *"Help me"* or *"Susie was here".* Behind the building lies the top of a concrete cistern known to survivors simply as "the Hole".

"They used to put kids down in there when they were bad" explained Geronimo Henry as we stood over the cistern.

"A lot of times they'd never come out of there alive. One day the staff just sealed it up. That's why we call this place the Mush Hole, not because of the mushy food. Down that Hole is nothing but mush now: those kids."

According to Geronimo and school records that I accessed, the surrounding land was filled with the graves of generations of students who had died in huge numbers for well over a century. Even John Zimmerman, Principal of the Mohawk Institute, admitted in a letter to the Indian Affairs Minister in the fall of 1949,

"It has been necessary to start burying the children two or three to a grave".

Our efforts to unearth this Holocaust got off to a good start. Under local pressure, the Confederacy chief Bill Montour let us use the tribal council's Ground Penetrating Radar (GPR) and a technician who interpreted the readings. Filmed by the local media and surrounded by a crowd of survivors and their families, we hit pay dirt immediately.

"You have huge soil displacements all over the site where children are reported to be buried. Those are not natural deposits. There's been a lot of digging going on in there" explained Clint King, the GPR technician employed by the Confederacy.

My own undergraduate training in archaeology helped the process at this stage, as did the aid of a forensic specialist from the Ontario Coroner's Office named Greg Olsen. Based on the GPR readings and Geronimo Henry's extensive testimony, we marked an area fifty yards east of the school for an initial test excavation.

On November 21, 2011, the first public excavation of a suspected Indian residential school grave site began. Two of the sponsoring Mohawk elders, Bill and Cheryl Squire, held a brief prayer ceremony and then opened the ground to commence the dig. Our dig team of five included me, Cheryl Squire, Geronimo Henry, a Mohawk videographer, and an accredited archaeologist. The Men's Fire security group stood by, smudging the area and holding back passersby.

My excavation notes from those days tell some of the story:

21 November. Day 1 at Test Dig Site A:
Commencing at A1 Unit of 275 square meters with 1-meter increments. (Grid Map 014)

Level 1: Excavated to a depth of 35 centimeters. Unearthed charcoal, brick, bits of bone and teeth, the bottom of a shoe sole. Material saturated with crumbly white substance, possibly potash or lime used to decay buried remains. Bones comprised two sizeable fragments identified as the vertebrae and humerus of a young child approx. 1.2 meters in height.

22 November. Day 2 at same site: Excavated to a depth of 55 centimeters. Quickly found charcoal deposits and many bone fragments, teeth and children-sized buttons. Latter were not plastic but of a pre-1950 style made of wood or bone/abalone shell. The same style buttons were found at Glebe burial site 2.2 kilometers from the school and were positively identified as coming from Mush Hole school uniforms from the 1930's or '40's.

23 November. Day 3 at same site: Excavated to a depth of 75 centimeters. Many of the same buttons found with charcoal and bone fragments, along with bits of a green and blue blanket spotted with rust coloration, possibly blood. Large bones found at 60 centimeters, possibly pig bones but cut at sharp angles. Mixed with these was a human bone identified as a small joint socket, knee or hip, from a child one meter in height. Socket bone found close to base of tree where buttons also found.

24 November. Day 4 at same site: Key discovery! The tree's roots exposed to 70 centimeters reveal same buttons and bone pieces tangled in roots. This confirmed GH's description of school practice of planting trees on remains of children. Bone identified as fragment of human tibia from child approx. 1.3 meters in height.

Emotions were running high at this point, once the Mohawks learned that children's bones had been positively identified. The dig was suspended to give people a chance to reflect and talk. Some of the elders began to lose their nerve, influenced, as it turned out, by tribal council agents who bribed and coerced people to drop away from our work.

And on the second day of our dig, the Confederacy chief Bill Montour withdrew his support for our work after being called to Ottawa by his paymasters.

At that point I felt the writing was on the wall for our investigation and our window of opportunity was closing. And so, with the permission of the sponsoring elders, I sent the bones we'd unearthed to the Smithsonian Institute in Washington, D.C. for positive confirmation. I also asked one of our consultants, Greg Olsen of the Provincial Coroner's Office, for his opinion. He insisted that we continue.

"I'd stake my reputation that this is from a young girl" Olsen said to me as he was filmed holding up the socket bone that we unearthed on Day Three.

"I'm applying for a Coroner's injunction so we can access the Anglican Church records and do a thorough dig of the whole area."

Greg never got his chance. Soon after he was given a severe "talking to" by his government bosses and dropped away. He told me by phone that he had been prohibited from participating in the dig, even in his spare time. That was just the opening salvo.

Over Christmas the Anglican Church, Bill Montour and the feds moved quickly to destroy our work.

By the new year of 2012, the entire Mush Hole investigation had been effectively derailed. All the original sponsoring elders save Bill and Cheryl Squire reneged on their written promise to support our work after a series of bribes and threats had been issued to them. The usual smears and rumors about me began to be spread among the Mohawks in the same manner I'd so often experienced.

Not surprisingly, the standard media blackout accompanied this shutdown. Not a single Canadian media outlet reported what we had achieved: the first time in Canadian history that the remains of children from an Indian residential school gravesite had been uncovered and positively identified.

But light continued to appear. A Smithsonian forensic expert named Dr. Don Ortner contacted me to confirm that two of our thirteen bone fragments were indeed human. And an Anglican Church insider named Leona Moses reached out to us and asked for a meeting. Cheryl Squire and I met her in her home on the local Mohawk reserve.

"Bishop Bob Bennett threatened me yesterday" Leona described to us over tea on January 9, 2012.

"He said if I ever disclosed what I knew about the Mush Hole records I'd end up in jail 'or worse'. Those were his exact words."

As an Anglican Church researcher for ten years, Leona had stumbled across something in that church's archives at Huron College known as the "G-12 series". It contained *stuff that could bring down the church",* according to Leona, including accounts of secret experiments conducted on Mohawk children over a century, statistics showing enormous death rates in the Mush Hole of as much as 75%, and reports of child trafficking and "cultic rituals" performed on children in the Mush Hole basement.

Equally explosive, Leona had also uncovered in the G-12 collection a written agreement to wipe out the Mohawk Nation that dated from 1870. It was signed by top officials of the British Crown, the New England Society that ran the school, and the local non-Mohawk tribes.

"This is a smoking gun pointing to genocide" Leona explained. But she was terrified of Bishop Bennett from the Anglican Huron Diocese and what he might do to her.

Leona's fears were justified. Neither the smoking gun nor she herself lasted long. A year later, her house burned down, destroying all her evidence. Soon after that she died of unexplained causes that nobody who knew her wanted to discuss.

Nevertheless, the Mohawk children's graves had been opened. Despite our shut down, the truth that we had unearthed was now out in the public realm. And that evidence would have a huge impact that same year in the Common Law Court of Justice trial in Europe that eventually forced the resignation of Pope Benedict and other criminals of Church and State.

As always, as one door was closed, another one had been opened.

....

The fact that a person who committed an act which constitutes a crime under international law acted as a Head of State or responsible government official does not relieve him of responsibility under international law.
– Principle Three of the <u>Nuremberg Legal Principles</u>, United Nations, 1950

Joseph Ratzinger was not a happy camper as the year 2012 unfolded.

Like a beleaguered Richard Nixon in his final days, "Joe the Rat" (as he was known among his fellow Catholic Cardinals) felt the hangman approaching. Ratzinger had made a lot of enemies over the years, especially when as a Cardinal he had been the Vatican's head Thought Policeman who rooted out church reformers. Becoming "Pope Benedict" hadn't made things any better, especially when he tried concealing the Mafia connection to Vatican finances. A palace coup masterminded by his own Secretary of State, Tarciscio Bertone, was moving quickly to have him ousted from his gilded papal "throne". Even his own butler, Paolo Gabriele, had leaked the guy's secret journal to the Italian press and been tossed in a Vatican prison for it.

It was the perfect time for us to strike at the oldest criminal syndicate on our planet.

I had wanted to go after the guy ever since I had witnessed the enormous popular opposition against him at the 20,000-strong "Protest the Pope" march in London in the summer of 2010. Ratzinger was the perfect symbol of papal criminality; he even looked like the Evil Emperor.

Even more to the point, critical new evidence against him was given to our Tribunal soon after the Mush Hole dig was shut down, from insiders in the Anglican and Catholic churches. It involved something called the Ninth Circle.

Two survivors of this cult – which had been formed by the Jesuits in the 18th century to control heads of state and popes – had come forward in 2011 to describe its murderous rites of torturing, killing and cannibalizing children. These Dutch survivors, Toos Neijenhuis and Anne Marie van Blijenburgh, provided our ITCCS with a close-up view of how the intergenerational cult operated. Others gave us a bigger picture of the Ninth Circle's relationship to organized crime, governments, and churches.

As it turns out, Catholic and Anglican orphanages and schools have traditionally been a hotspot for Ninth Circle ritual killings. And one of these cult killing sites named by several of our sources was, low and behold, the Anglican Church's "Mush Hole" school in Canada.

The first hint of this link came from an official in the Anglican Primate's head office in Toronto. This source was shocked and troubled by our surfacing of the Mush Hole remains during 2011 and wrestled with an obvious guilty conscience. According to this source,

"Last year, Primate Fred Hiltz was directed by a secret communique from Archbishop of Canterbury Justin Welby to destroy any evidence linking British Royal Family members or any Catholic or Anglican prelate to the death or disappearance of children at the Mohawk school. The Archbishop specifically asked that a search be done in the same records for The Circle of Nine or something like that."

A source within the Vatican went even further when he spoke to me in the spring of 2012.

"There are references to the Ninth Circle in the closed files of the Magisterium's Office going back as far as the year 1722. I noted an insert made in August of 1908 that describes the Circle gathering for a 'sabot ritual' at a Church of England Mohawk school in Ontario where 'the sanctified' were ritually flayed and sacrificed. That's their code word for children to be killed."

A police-accredited psychic from Nanaimo named Yvonne Fantin accompanied us during the early phase of our work at the Mush Hole. Yvonne gave many vivid descriptions of witnessing the ritual killings of native children taking place in a closed, sub-basement area of the Mohawk Institute in Brantford. As she described on film in 2011,

"There were both Anglicans and Catholics in that basement crypt each time, always wearing the same purple and red robes. They were skinning children alive and eating their body parts. It was like they were trying out new ways to prolong torture and terror in young children to control their minds and their souls too. Like a big experiment."

These same tortures are commonplace practices at Ninth Circle rituals held today in Europe, according to the eyewitnesses Toos Neijenhuis and Anne Marie van Blijenburgh.

The fact that Joseph Ratzinger had met in private conference with Queen Elizabeth at Holyrood Castle during his 2010 visit to England was not lost on our people or the world media. But few people realized that the agreement made by those two Ninth Circle members reunified the Roman Catholic and Anglican churches and thereby bound them to the same practices of child killing and its concealment.

Armed with this knowledge and the voluminous evidence I had amassed on the Vatican's key role in the Canadian genocide, the ITCCS established an International Common Law Court of Justice during the summer of 2012. And at the top of its list of thirty defendants to be summoned were Joseph Ratzinger and Elizabeth Windsor.

The formal charges in the indictment were twofold: plotting and engaging in Crimes against Humanity, and actively concealing the same crimes.

Joe and Liz were not the only people in our crosshairs. Twenty-eight top officials of Church, State and Business were also named in the Court indictment, including some of those responsible for the Indian residential school atrocities in Canada. All these co-conspirators were summoned to appear before the opening session of the Common Law Court on July 18, 2012 in Brussels.

Not surprisingly, none of these accused replied to the Summons or appeared before the Court. But this worked in our favor, for the abstaining of the accused allowed the Magistrates and the Jury to infer that the defendants were not disputing or challenging the charges made against them and thereby were pleading to a *"pro confesso"* guilt.*

....

*PRO CONFESSO, *for confessed.* When the defendant has been served personally with a subpoena, or when not being so served has appeared and afterwards neglects to answer the matter contained in the bill, it shall be *pro confesso,* as if the matter were confessed by the defendant. (from *Black's Law Dictionary*).
See www.murderbydecree.com , "ITCCS Archives".

On the basis of their tacit admission of guilt, and the overwhelming evidence linking the defendants with the deaths of more than 60,000 children in Canadian Indian residential schools, the jury by a unanimous vote found all the defendants guilty *in absentia* and sentenced them to life imprisonment. The process took seven months, as the evidence was weighed, and the defendants were given a continual opportunity to respond. The verdict was pronounced on February 25, 2013.

But by then we had already made history again. Two weeks earlier, the prime defendant in the case, Pope Benedict, had resigned from his papal office. In truth, we had pushed him out.

Here is how the recipe worked: Take one Spanish career diplomat named Eduardo Gutierrez Buruaga who is on the payroll of a soon-to-be pope named Jorge ("Francis") Bergoglio. Add in a Ratzinger-hating Vatican politician named Tarcisio Bertone and stir slightly. Then mix in all our ITCCS evidence linking Rat Boy with the Ninth Circle and its Mafia funders, bake it for a few days and presto! You have one succulently deposed pope, quicker than you can say Rodrigo Borgia.

We in the ITCCS had learned about the move to depose Ratzinger and knew exactly where to place the loaded gun we carried. Early in the new year, our docket of evidence was delivered by one of our people to Eduardo Gutierrez de Buruaga.

On February 6, 2012, five days before Ratzinger resigned from office, Gutierrez de Buruaga used what we gave him. As the Ambassador of Spain to the Vatican and under the orders of the future pope Jorge Bergoglio, de Buruaga delivered a diplomatic note to the Vatican Secretary of State and his co-conspirator Tarcisio Bertone. The note said that Pope Benedict could face arrest in Spain because of his personal complicity in "disturbing incidents".

Barely a week later, Joseph Ratzinger stepped down from his office: the first papal resignation in over six centuries.

But Gutierrez de Buruaga did not stop there. He worked with Bertone to swing Cardinals' votes in the papal election towards Jorge Bergoglio. He also diverted attention from Bergoglio's involvement in Ninth Circle killings and child trafficking under the Argentine military junta during its Dirty Wars.

Buruaga's own family had been similarly complicit in such Vatican-sponsored crimes under the Franco dictatorship in Spain, so he had a personal interest in concealing the crime.

Joseph Ratzinger was the perfect fall guy for everyone concerned. By bringing attention to the Ninth Circle he had to serve as a public scapegoat, even as the smiley-faced "Pope Francis" was ushered into the papacy to do damage control and distract from the wider actors in the crime.

Our evidence had been a key weapon in this coup d'etat designed by Bergoglio, Bertone and de Buruaga. The latter stayed on as the Spanish Ambassador to the Vatican and Bertone was safely pensioned off six months later.

Who had used who? Frankly, it was a mutual effort. The deposing of Pope Benedict was an objectively joint operation by the Bergoglio faction and our movement, but for entirely different purposes. Our point had been made. We had demonstrated how the people can depose the powerful by relying on their own actions and Common Law proceedings.

We had also proven the ancient adage that the enemy of my enemy can be a temporary ally.

Building on our victory, which many people still find difficult to understand or accept, we convened a second Common Law court in the summer of 2014, this time focused strictly on the Ninth Circle. As part of those proceedings, the Court issued a Public Summons to the new Pope Francis, Jesuit leader Adolfo Pachon and Archbishop of Canterbury Justin Welby, who had ordered the destruction of the Mush Hole evidence in Canada. All three of the men were top Ninth Circle participants.

Within two weeks of receiving the Court Summons, Jesuit Adolfo Pachon – who as the "Black Pope" was one of five head officiants of the Ninth Circle – suddenly resigned from his office. So, in truth, our second Court action eventually deposed both the official and unofficial heads of the Church of Rome.

Throughout the second trial, the Court presented its evidence about the accused, including their presence at Ninth Circle killings in Wales, Belgium and France. Once again, none of the accused replied and thereby admitted guilt by *Pro Confesso.*

The Court eventually found all three men guilty as charged, of ongoing Crimes against Humanity. Common Law Arrest Warrants were issued against them and the smiley "Pope Francis" was nearly apprehended by Common Law Sheriffs on two occasions. And for years after, the Vatican once more plunged into global damage control and obfuscation of the criminal conviction of its top officials.

Everything was different after that.

Chapter Eight: Coming of Age in Kanata

I was agreeably surprised when I came here to discover what a rich land it is. You can grow corn, wheat, and any kind of crop with hardly any dung. Here there are no game wardens or lords over you, no poor laws, scarcely any taxes. This is a land of liberty and plenty where we are held in esteem by our neighbours. We aim to keep it that way.
– Philip Annett, Upper Canada farmer and participant in the 1837 Rebellion, in a letter to his relatives in Wiltshire, England, March 30, 1824

None of us are obligated to hold allegiance to a foreign criminal regime like the Crown of England. Its authority has rested on a false jurisdiction violently imposed on all of us. If we are ever to wipe away the stain of genocide in Canada it will only happen through a Republic that reclaims the land and its wealth for all the people within a federation of equal nations. We must recover the dream of equality of our ancestors.
– Kevin Annett in a speech delivered to the Founding Convention of the Republican Party of Kanata, Winnipeg, January 15, 2015

All these battles fairly won had left me feeling like an exile who had earned the right of return. In truth, there was no home for me to go back to.

Despite having been vindicated by events and the evidence, I remained a pariah in my own country, at least at the official level: blacklisted, shunned, and erased from the memory of the nation. The Empire remained intact, if shaken, and could no more acknowledge me or my legacy than it could take responsibility for the horror it had committed.

But all of that was just the appearance of things. Beneath the entrenched lie and the board room agendas churned the real state of the nation in countless towns and villages or sheltering from the night behind downtown city dumpsters. Returning to Canada in the fall of 2014, I encountered sharp discontent everywhere, but especially within me.

Had it been enough? Was there more I had to do? The answer stared back at me as plainly as the eyes of a survivor, or the words of Wolf-Dieter Zimmerman, a pastor of the anti-Nazi Confessing Church:

"I could no longer bear the shame of calling myself a citizen and associating with a nation soaked in the blood of innocents. I refused that association and its complicity by finding a new identity among those who had been condemned to death by my government. Along with them, I looked to a new nation that would arise from out of our sacrifice, cleansed of mass murder and lies, and worthy of the righteous."

That sentiment consumed me in the wake of my twenty-year long campaign. I could not in good conscience associate any longer with Canada. The source of its sickness had to be expunged for its slaughters were continuing. Then I remembered that the vision of what could replace Canada had been gifted to me already by one of my ancestors: a farmer and blacksmith named Philip Annett who was my great-great-great Grandfather.

Philip had come from England in 1820 and settled with his family on land near what is now Watford, Ontario. His letters to other relatives in England brimmed with a joyous enthusiasm for the "land of liberty and plenty" he had discovered.

Settlers like Philip Annett had found their home and were determined to hold on to it. They shared the land in peace with the local Chippewa Indians and fought incursions of British colonial speculators and Anglican Bishops who hungered for the same land. And one day in the winter of 1837, Philip and his neighbours took up arms to overthrow Crown authority and establish what William Lyon McKenzie called "a Republic of Free and Equal Peoples".

Sadly, our homegrown revolution was crushed by Tory militia. Somehow Philip Annett survived the hangman and deportation, and with his wife Sarah he raised six sons, including James, who begat Calvin, who begat Ross, who begat William, who begat me. Through our blood line has persisted the dream of a Republic in Canada: what the traditional Six Nations still call the Two Row Wampum of Equality between our nations.

We call it Kanata. And in the new year of 2015, I gathered in convention with two hundred people in Winnipeg to make the dream a reality by forming the basis for such a Republic. Sixty thousand murdered children had led me there.

"Kanata" is a Haudenosaunee word meaning *"our village"*, or more exactly *"where the people sit as one around the council fire"*. People gather in that way naturally as free-born men and women, and government and economics and the law and religion operate that way in a free society.

But Canada has always operated in the opposite way, by the rule of the few over the many: by the whims of Executive Orders in Council, of foreign financiers, of a corrupt judiciary and a puppet Parliament owing its sole allegiance to a doddering idiot in London. What else but continued lies and bloodshed must attend it all? For it is this political arrangement that caused the Canadian Genocide and compels it to continue.

Turning sixty years of age prodded me to take up where my ancestor Philip had left off. For too long, my determination to see justice done for the innocent caused me to become type cast within a single issue of residential school victims. But the time had come for my natural political bent to renew itself on a broader field of action.

After our second successful conviction of Vatican criminals during 2014, I knew it was time to bring the battle home to the scene of the crime. Besides, I have always loved kicking the biggest butt in town, and there is no more tempting a target than the institution and idea of monarchy. So, declaring for the Republic in Canada and working to establish it as an alternative to the bloody legacy of "the Crown" seemed to be the next obvious step for me, building on my struggles and our campaigns over the previous decades.

A lot of people in Canada agreed with me: nearly 60% of them, who when polled in 2014 said they want an end to any ties with the British monarchy. We also had affirmation from International Law, that states that a government that commits crimes against humanity has no right to expect allegiance from its citizens.

Something unseen brought the two hundred of us together in 2015 to establish the vision and the first steps towards the Republic of Kanata. It was no accident that we gathered in Winnipeg, which has always been the unstated heartland of our nation and the source of repeated efforts to rebel.

On the first day of our Kanata Convention, our delegates stood at Louis Riel's grave in St. Boniface and remembered.

A new spirit animated all our words and decisions. Our event was not your usual political convention. We spoke not of electioneering but taking back our local communities; not of voting away our authority to others but reclaiming it through Republican Peoples' Assemblies. But imagining let alone taking such steps requires a personal quality missing in many people: the capacity to take responsibility for oneself and one's world in the face of a growing corporate tyranny.

My Metis relatives embodied that spirit of self-reliance when they called themselves *Oo-tee-pem-soo-uck*, which means, *"The people who own themselves"*. That is a hard concept and an even more difficult practice for many Canadians, who for generations have been born and bred into colonial servitude as "subjects" of a foreign monarch. The idea of self-governance, that the people are the source of sovereignty and authority, is the basis of our vision of Kanata. But this Republican principle is a treasonable notion within "official" Canada.

Nevertheless, over the years that followed our formation of a Republican movement, we struggled in a hundred different communities to make that vision a reality.

We issued a Public Proclamation that declared our sovereign independence from the British Crown and offered citizenship to people who renounced their allegiance to that foreign power. We established local Republican Assemblies and broadcast our message through a new radio program called *Radio Free Kanata* – and later renamed *Here We Stand*. We replaced "Crown" legal authority by creating Common Law Courts and Republican Sheriffs to enforce their warrants and verdicts.

Naturally, many of these first efforts failed. Our resources were meager and our numbers too few. We learned firsthand the unwillingness of people to risk and embrace a revolutionary change in the absence of a working alternative to the status quo - something they can safely belong to. Even the most enthusiastic Republicans have retained a "wait and see" attitude to the movement, expecting someone else to bring in the new society for them.

If I thought that child torture and genocide were tough mental sledding for most people in Canada, it pales in comparison to their reaction to the idea that they are free to take the law and political authority into their own hands. They do not seem capable of even imagining doing so.

In his own campaign to free his people from their servitude to the British Empire, Mohandas Gandhi observed that without winning their mental and spiritual independence from that power, genuine political sovereignty would be impossible, since the Indians would simply replicate the old masters in new form. History proved him right.

Canadians have still not come of age or won their independence. They don't know how to do so, having missed the liberating catharsis of revolution and civil war that cuts the umbilical cord to the past and allows a new self-definition.

Ruled and bled by successive Empires, dependent on foreign markets and agendas, our country's objective condition was best summed up in the 18th century by the mistress of Louis XIV, Madame de Pompadour, when she declared,

"Canada exists only to provide me with furs."

Replace the latter with fish and timber, then wheat, oil, uranium and natural gas, and change the speaker to the British, then the Americans, and now the Chinese, and you will have a concise and accurate economic history of Canada.

Our political condition has stayed equally retarded and colonized, ruled as we are by a Governor-General appointed by a foreign monarch to whom every politician, cop, judge and civil servant takes an oath of personal loyalty. Such a dependent animus imbues our entire culture, producing the deadly but accurate cliché of the terminally "nice" Canadian who will sacrifice anything, including his ethics and convictions, rather than upset authority and convention.

In many ways, Canadians are just like the Indians they made into enslaved "wards of the state", stuck in infancy without a legal or sovereign personality. Canada is invisible to the rest of the world, and especially to America, because in a real sense it does not exist. It is not a nation that was born as much as an arrangement that was made.

Never having found its own identity, Canada's maturation has remained arrested, like a toddler who never learns to move and think freely or develop an individuated personality.

Coming home to such political infantilism after having unsettled the oldest criminal power in the world made my ostracism by my own people easier to bear. I discovered the broad view and learned not take Canada too seriously, especially as I encountered once again the smug self-satisfaction possessed by Canucks of every political stripe.

Struggle as I did to raise the banner of the Republic of Kanata in the face of the endemic fear and caution of Canadians, I knew that my efforts were for now like tossing seeds onto parched prairie soil. It might take many seasons and storms for any of them to sprout.

In the meantime, I began to chronicle all that I had done.

....

Over the next four years I wrote ten books. My tomes included all my research on Church-State genocide in Canada, several biographical pieces, the case for the Republic of Kanata and a series of "how to" manuals on Common Law and surviving as a whistleblower. I also crafted a play called "The Land of No-One", which showed the impact of the medical extermination of Indian children on the life of one of the Canadian families responsible for it.

Despite its "controversial" theme, the play was enthusiastically picked up on two occasions by theatre companies in Duncan, B.C. and Toronto, during 2017 and 2018. Both times, the play was shut down before it could be produced. While none of the erstwhile supporters of cast and crew wanted to say why they suddenly bailed on the play, its extinguishing was undoubtedly caused by the same forces that routinely cause my books to vanish without a trace from libraries across Canada.

This shutdown campaign can reach ludicrous proportions. In the spring of 2019, one of my supporters in the small town of Owen Sound, Ontario booked me in to the local library to read from my latest book *The Border*. Two days later, my friend called me up in a very distraught state to say that the library had cancelled my event.

"The head librarian said they didn't approve of you as the author" he said.

"When I pressed her why, she actually admitted that she'd been instructed not to allow you to speak and not to carry your books."

Ah, the joys of the Blacklist. Oddly, these incidents have bothered me less the more they've happened. In fact, I have learned to take inspiration from such persecution, in the attitude of the native man who told me long ago in a healing circle in Nanaimo,

"If you got canned by the United Church, you must have done something right!".

Being under a big boot can crush us or raise us to new heights. Repression and personal loss have elevated me. Rather than feeling discouraged by being attacked and marginalized, I learned that such unrelenting repression is the lot of anyone who poses a genuine threat to the system. Joe Hendsbee taught me that when I was eighteen.

The old guy used to take delight in recounting as battle honors the litany of firings, assaults and smear campaigns he had endured for half a century. These unrelenting attacks were reassuring to him at the end of his life because they were the living proof that he had never sold out or given up, and that he still had the bad guys worried.

Now that is something our supposedly powerful enemies don't understand: that all their arrows and calculated venom aimed our way only help us over the long run because they keep us strong and our example and memory alive. Provided we don't ever give up, our corporate adversaries don't know how to handle us. And so short of killing us, which just creates a martyr and an enduring place for us in history, they can only use their fixed methods of trying to isolate and discredit us. Fighting their system is really like engaging with a stuck record. And anything stuck can be outmaneuvered.

I learned this from time and suffering, and have tried to pass on what I know to younger people. But the young have been somewhat less than willing to listen, and not simply because of their preoccupation with mind-numbing technologies.

For as another good buddy of mine named Antonio Gramsci pointed out from within one of Benito Mussolini's fascist prisons in 1937,

"Illusion is the most tenacious quality of the human mind. History teaches but it has no pupils."

Our own experience is always our best teacher. But none of us have been taught to believe in ourselves or our own judgements and lessons. In many of the Common Law and Republic workshops that I conduct with people, the first question I pose to them is this:

"What have you learned?".

And then I ask them,

"How are you applying what you've learned in your own life?".

The rest is up to them. But that step requires a self-reliance that is still foreign to most people. Continually I am asked,

"Okay Kevin, I agree with you, but what do we do next?"

"That's for you to answer" I reply.

Their response to my challenge is the litmus test that separates the chosen ones from the herd. A few people know what to do and go about doing it. They become the spark that ignites others, often unintentionally. But they are only a very few.

I have spent my recent years seeking out that remnant. Most of them are in hiding, often from themselves. A few of those few remain public and clear-sighted, and resolved to fight the Thing to the death. But over time and from their many wounds, these warriors become hard individualists, unable to believe that trusting and working with others like them will yield anything but more defeat.

In fairness, I find the same distrust in me: one of the downsides of having had too much experience. With growing awareness of what we face comes a world weariness that can immobilize the best of us. Even love must rest, wrote Byron.

That said, my life, like New York City, somehow keeps managing to continue.

I have been blessed throughout my years with a sense of high purpose and resolve that's brought me through the worst of times. But as well, and even as a boy, I have enjoyed an inner peace and equilibrium that intensified the older I became and has remained unaffected by circumstance. I call this the ability to find the eternity that is present in each moment. As an aged man I have appreciated the advice of Marcus Aurelius, who urged us to find our recreation and recovery within the sanctuary of our own mind. All else seems secondary, like a passing wind outside our home.

Perhaps that is why it's been possible for me to chronicle all my battles. In the created written word translated from our deepest heart, the corruption and madness of the world has no place. To create, to find meaning, to love completely and to fight to the end for who and what we love: these are our very human answers to the Great Cosmic Shrug. Without them, we become the well-clad ghost people who wander city streets and daily routine in a journey that leads nowhere.

The Republic we imagine begins as a place for the righteous remnant, the realm of eternity that Jesus spoke of and ushered into the world by becoming it. Like our virtues and our failings, that new nation cannot be denied even if it cannot be perceived.

Epilogue: The Fork in the Resurrection Road

We who lived in concentration camps can remember the men who walked through the huts comforting others, giving away their last piece of bread. They may have been few in number, but they offer sufficient proof that everything can be taken from a man but one thing: the last of the human freedoms - to choose one's attitude in any given set of circumstances, to choose one's own way.

— Viktor E. Frankl, *Man's Search for Meaning*

All the nations will be gathered before him, and he will separate the people one from another as a shepherd separates the sheep from the goats.

– Matthew 25:32

The other night I knelt next to a forgotten box of memories and discovered a folder of my daughters' drawings and letters from their early years. Among the treasures was a birthday card to me from Clare, inscribed *"To a speshul dad from a speshul girl"*, and Elinor's first crayon scrawls attempting to form themselves into human figures. Then my eyes fell on a newspaper clipping that had inexplicably found its way into the memorabilia. It was entitled:

"Babies were buried under the apple trees: Grim residential school stories finally surface".

William Wordsworth observed that a lowly flower *"can give thoughts that do often lie too deep for tears."* In my case, it was a news account from 1998 that did the trick.

My silent heart that languished beyond the reach of tears and lamentation burst forth in that moment, as I recalled that even though it cost me my life I could no more have abandoned those little ones who were tossed into secret graves than I could my own children. And that recognition drove from me all my accumulated regret and shadow, to fall away like an unwanted skin as a new path opened before me.

I had a very real foreshadowing of this shift in me many years ago, in my Port Alberni congregation. One of my burly logger-parishioners asked me in a Bible study class why I was always going on about Jesus' account of the Final Judgement found in Matthew Chapter 25.

I replied,

"Because it's the only time in scripture that Jesus says clearly where you can find him, and that's out among the outcasts and the unwanted. What you deny to them you deny to him. Jesus doesn't just identify with the poor; he's saying that he is the neglected one."

"And so if we don't feed the poor we're going to hell, right?" he remarked sourly.

"If we do the wrong thing then we end up lessening ourselves, and we're diminished inside" I said.

"That eventually extinguishes our moral substance and yes, it creates a void that is hell, inside us and around us in the world. But we can choose to be otherwise and follow our conscience, like taking the other fork in a road."

"That's what Jesus meant by the sheep getting separated from the goats? So, we're supposed to be the sheep, right?"

My logger friend paused and added gruffly,

"That makes sense, Rev. But ain't it the sheep that get sacrificed?"

Watch out what you pray for, in other words.

Life shows us that if you let your light shine, you will become even more of a target. Jesus does not address that paradoxical risk, besides saying we should gladly bear it. People may talk of doing the right thing, but how many are willing to accept its consequences and go all the way to the Cross?

Once abstract, these matters became dangerously real for me after I took that fork in the road and the great divide in my life increased.

Allowing my light to no longer mingle with shadow but step away and stand upright placed me on the spiritual radar of the dark ruler of this world and plunged me into unending battle with it. I found that this struggle made me increasingly invisible to the worldly-bound people around me. Those whom I once called family and friends faded, along with the power that runs them, until they became as insubstantial as what I once thought was my world. And I became as much a ghost to them.

This strange experience has been an unexpected but sublime journey into exile, a quarter century of consequences whose lessons are hard and clear.

One of those lessons is the recognition that regardless of the sacrifice we make or the victory that we win, the world forgets it all, because it never understood.

Thus, I am led inexorably elsewhere.

....

It is natural for someone approaching the age of sixty-five to think that the world is ending. Take Dan the Man, for instance.

Recently, Dan and I had a wonderfully unexpected reunion after a pause of forty years. The door to a Cambie street bus opened and there he was at the wheel, bearing the same smile and much grey hair.

Dan Schwarzfeld had been my best friend in our latter days of high school until we went our own separate ways. During those brief teenage years that seem in hindsight to constitute decades, Dan and I were bonded by our quirkiness: me for instigating protests and him for obsessing over vampires, UFO's and film making. We once spent a weekend riding our ten-speed bikes in the rain to Vancouver Island just to check out a report of a UFO sighting in Duncan that had not happened.

Over beers in Gastown during a break on his split-shift, Dan talked about his impending retirement from bus driving. Soon the subject turned to death.

"I've been living on borrowed time ever since that fucking terrorist nearly blew us up" Dan muttered.

He was referring to the historic incident at Paris' Orly airport in 1972 when Carlos The Jackel fired a rocket-propelled grenade at the El Al plane that was carrying the entire Schwarzfeld clan to a family reunion in Tel Aviv. And missed.

"Sure, he fucking missed!" exclaimed Dan when I reminded him.

"That's not the point. You never forget shit like that. And now I'm retiring, for God's sake. I'm sixty-five next month, can you fucking believe it? Things are over for me, man."

I didn't bother telling Dan very much about my own life. Too much had happened, most of it beyond any of his reference points. We shook hands and agreed jokingly to do it again in another forty years.

It's always hard to say goodbye to the past.

Grey hairs and exploding planes notwithstanding, the funny thing is that things <u>are</u> ending. A society as violently dissociated as ours cannot survive itself, nor should we bother prolonging it. And yet despite my lifelong aversion to the whole sick arrangement, for too many of my years I have tried changing the system without realizing that it is irredeemable. For civilization as we know it is a permanent war of humanity against itself, against nature and against God. And every war must in the end expend itself into ashes and ruin.

A specifically Biblical view of the present COVID-inspired global police state is that it is nothing less than a divine judgement on our way of life and its inherent sickness, idolatry, and fear. The genocide we inflicted on others has now blown back to claim us as well. But, gee folks: what else is new?

Of course, human disasters can yield remnants who endure and birth a new world. That is the claim of most religions, as well as our personal yearning for immortality. The problem with most "sacred" beliefs is that they're espoused by old men who feel compelled to draw hopeful conclusions because their own mortal coil is winding down.

Knowing our species' historic incapacity to stop its own self-ravaging, it is probably a moot question to ask why it's that important for humans to survive themselves. I doubt that Mother Earth will shed many tears once we succumb.

What I have learned from life is that there remains an unbreachable chasm between the love that births us and the life we end up leading.

Enigmatically, love never becomes more than a personal impulse. It doesn't ever constitute the operating principle and motive force of any society. Individually we are usually angels but collectively always a demon. That discontinuity is absolute, and it creates an existential absurdity that has tragic consequences. But all of it seems to be completely unreal: a chimeric illusion of no substance.

Even more to the point is that the transitory nature of so-called reality is totally incongruent with the unchanging nature of the love that is as inherent to us as our own self-awareness. Everything changes, except the impulse of our hearts: as if an eternal substance is trapped forever in a chaos of unreality and illusion.

This dissociated existence suggests that one of two things is at work in humanity. Either a massive group psychosis is going on, or (and this is the more intriguing and simpler explanation) we do not actually exist - at least, not as we have imagined.

Suffering gives us the opportunity to pierce the veil of illusion that cocoons us. If we are beaten and battered long enough and prevented from returning to what we consider is our normal life, the veil can fade and even vanish. And then, beyond all the imagined boundaries, something of truth can dawn.

Truth, of course, is like romance: something very wonderful until its consequences cause the bubble to burst. The more we stare our life in the face, the less real most of it becomes, as in quantum physics when sub-atomic particles disappear the more that we observe them. What stays real is our sense of being and the lessons we experience.

This phenomenon suggests that while we seem to exist in our own self-consciousness, we don't exist in any measurably objective sense. So how can we know what is true in a world of illusion?

In fact, we cannot know, according to the reigning Uncertainty paradigm, because there is no such thing as the Absolute, which is a construct of the human mind. Anything can appear to be true. Goodbye then to the hope that love or any moral principle or just law can come to govern society. Hello to the relativistic chaos that is causing our world to collapse because all our reference points have vanished.

The odd thing is that such a surrender to the void is comforting to traumatized people like us. I have seen that phenomenon played out most explicitly on psychiatric wards, but I witness that submission every day in the *"Well, this is the best I can hope for"* attitude of despair that both rich and poor cling to in their respective rabbit holes. But imposing such a ceiling over our psyches bars us from the liberty that comes with dying. At each step of the ruination of my old life, I felt that the best part of me was set free from an invisible dungeon. Then I could sense more of the truth that we all search for unconsciously, like a salmon driven by nature to seek its spawning grounds.

In the meantime, the horror of our relativistic age tries to strike us down at every turn. It is wrong for children to be killed by anyone, says our heart. It is wrong only when the killers are not priests or millionaires, says our world. The guilty need to be punished and stopped, says our heart. The guilty will be punished only when doing so won't step on somebody's big toes, says our world. Mass murder cannot be made better. Oh yes it can, answers the State, with enough money and words of "apology".

How can we do anything but fight on against the moral nothingness that poses as our society? But how long can we wage a seemingly unwinnable war against a void?

Choosing which fork in the road to take is the easy part.

....

"There was a young girl, she was pregnant, and she had her baby. Then they took it down into the kitchen where I was cooking with the nun. And the priest took that baby and threw it into the furnace alive. You could hear it cry out "Ahh!" and that little body went pop."

Irene Favel stared at the CBC reporter as she spoke those words, recounting tearfully what she had witnessed at the Muscowegan Catholic Indian residential school in Saskatchewan when she was ten years old. The female reporter gazed back at her blankly, without emotion.

How many times have I encountered the same obtuse indifference to our slaughter of children in the eyes and words of Canadians? Too often to recall. Moral and mental inertia is the norm, and therefore so too is the mass herd-like compliance with the present police state. But I am no longer alarmed at this as I once was. For now I recognize the condition of my people for what it is: that of the walking dead.

By that expression I don't mean those who have not yet been born. For I live among those whose group soul has been murdered by the same force that then acted through them to wipe out so many others, here in "The Land of No-One".

That term – "Terra Nullius" - was crafted by Roman rulers two millennia ago to apply to any land they wanted to conquer. It's a handy mental device to avoid seeing the people one is butchering.

Closer to our age, the same expression and idea was applied by Vatican lawyers as Rome first pillaged our continent. It referred to the place inhabited by any non-Catholic people. To the papacy, no-one can exist or be human outside its Church. Those who are not in their club are in a state of non-being and so their land is empty. They have forfeited their right to exist.

In truth, the term expresses the spiritual state of the conquerors themselves: that of a void that finds nothing wrong with killing children.

The hard truth is that the dead hand of the world's first corporation in Rome, metastasizing globally, has nearly killed anything alive or independent in our world. It is transforming all of humanity into dead component parts of its single, global machine. That extinction is nearly complete.

Just look around.

Having been raised in such living death, I didn't understand it until it turned on me. And in the agony that followed, something was born in me that allowed me to step out of the Necropolis I once called home.

My birth from death was a bloody severance. As I grow into my new life, I find that I am expelled ever more completely from the thoughts and considerations of the dead, just as they have no place in me anymore. For what does the light have in common with the night?

Recently in a TV interview, I described my long campaign to expose the Canadian genocide as a protest that became an exorcism that became a funeral service. The possessed body has died. It is past redemption.

That may be an unacceptable diagnosis to the dead and the dying, but it is the raw truth for those who are leaving the illusion and learning to take responsibility for what they know. Our Homo Sapiens species is being transformed into *Homo Machina*, a lifeform stripped of its human identity, liberty and gender, and as with any genocide, *incorporated* into a dead machine that is sucking all life from our mother Earth.

What then is to be done?

Perhaps the new extermination is obvious to more people now. But even the more "aware" among us cannot really accept that it is happening, if our present behaviour is any indication. We all cling to the past and deny the unacceptable. Of course, that's hardly an unusual response to approaching nightfall. I have often encountered it at death beds.

During my final year as a minister in Port Alberni, I was called to the local hospital to attend to a young woman named Carol who was in the terminal stage of cancer. Her husband Tony and the wider family were grouped around her bed, but they stood apart and avoided looking at her.

"She looks better today, don't you think?" offered Carol's mother.

"Yeah, yeah, she'll be her old self soon enough" replied Tony, fiddling with the bouquet of flowers resting on her nightstand.

I stood quietly as they carried on in that vein. Carol was too weak to speak or to even move her head. She was fading rapidly. Finally, I spoke up gently.

"It's getting near to the end. It's time to say your goodbyes".

The family turned on me with a common look of shock, and then anger.

"Bullshit! She's going to pull out of this thing!" spat the husband at me.

"She's dying, Tony. Just look at her" I answered.

The man turned his frightened eyes to his wife. And then after a moment he burst into tears, followed by all the others. A crushing weight seemed to lift from them. They drew close to Carol for the first time, hugging her gently and whispering in her ear. I touched the dying woman, said a silent prayer, and left.

I felt a deep peace on my way home and for the rest of that day, for I knew that Carol's passage would be easier now. But all her family avoided me after that. Tony even threw me a hateful stare the following week when we passed on the street. I had helped them ease her ending by telling them the truth about her condition, but they never forgave me for it - any more than can my culture for my reminding it of its own terminal condition.

How difficult it is for any of us who don't know our self to know that our time is over. And how even more arduous and hazardous for an entire nation and people to realize the same thing! How indeed, in this strange place that is still called Canada.

The truth is that it is time to summon those who we call dead back to life, by tossing a final shovel of soil on the tomb of all those "fat and greasy citizens" who pretend to live, and of the entity that owns them.

Presiding at the funeral of such an entity is not an easy thing to do when it is violently thrashing about in its death throes. The recent "public health measures" that banned public assemblies, free movement and unrestrained speech across the country are a sign of the funeral. The compliance of people with unreason and illusion is not what matters. The unreality of it all is the issue.

The question being so starkly posed now is whether even a remnant among us can learn to see through the illusions of death and stand unmoved in what is true. Will that remnant earn the right to endure and survive the nightfall that is upon us?

At the end of the day, I cannot believe that a people who have remained so unmoved by the slaughter of children in their midst – who are so unconnected to their own natures - are worthy of either liberty or survival.

Upon encountering our undeniable proof of the Indian residential schools extermination, a living people would have risen up and torn the murderers of Church and State limb from limb, if only to protect their own children and those who are to come. Instead, there has been only a bovine-like passivity and indifference among Canadians. Such is the behaviour of dead people.

Is there even one living soul still to be found in our lost city of Sodom?

And will even those who still live choose the fork in the road?

Postscript: In Times like These

I think it was Vladimir Lenin who observed that a single day of experiencing real events teaches us more than a decade of theorizing. This truth has struck home with a vengeance as I finish these words during the late spring of 2020.

The sound of military helicopter flyovers provided a fitting backdrop this morning as a street guy asked me why the Vancouver Public Library was closed.

"It's the flu virus scare" I replied, wondering where all the helicopters were going.

"Goddamned morons believe any crap that's fed to 'em" snorted my companion.

"For awhile" I replied.

Ever since my early baptism into radical politics after the Chilean military coup in 1973, I have often pondered how I would respond when the Big Boot came crashing down on lovely Canada. The refugees from the Chilean blood bath taught me a lot. Recent events have taught me more, especially how the Boot is being inflicted on us by none other than we ourselves. As the old joke goes,

"How do you get Canadians to jump into a vat of acid?"

"Easy. Just tell them to".

Ultimately, Canadians' present hysteria about the allegedly "new" police state is lost on me. None of these measures are new; they just haven't been practiced on any of us before.

Ever live on an Indian reservation? For many years you needed a pass to leave it and you had to report your movements to the RCMP. You still can't refuse vaccinations or any medical treatment if you're a reservation Indian. The cops can bust down your door and drag you and your kids away at any time, if you're an aboriginal. Or if you're any poor person, for that matter.

The same goes for America or any other nation. As good old Walt Whitman wrote in 1857,

"For this America is nothing but you and me. Its laws and statutes come from you and me; its crimes and its promise, its depredations and wars, its glory and its liberties, all from ourselves ..."

The monster that is stalking our land emerged from us. If the Final Solution of an absolutist Security State is a chipped, controlled, and imprisoned people, that extinguishment of liberty is something we chose over the risks of remaining free souls. We have become our own victims, just as the first casualty of Christianity was Jesus Christ himself.

On the other hand, the times are nothing if not comical.

After all, what is funnier than seeing fifty people standing in line protectively grasping rolls of toilet paper as they are scrutinized by store security guards?

Or watching passersby practice the latest way of shaking hands by tapping their feet to another's?

This is true Theatre of the Absurd. Or maybe we've all just gone psychotic.

In the spirit of the times, I am expected these days to pick my own explanation of the contrived COVID madness as I would a Flavor of the Month:

Big Pharma's latest Angst Campaign to boost its mega-profits?

China's power grab to crash the North American economy and pick up the pieces?

An Illuminati scheme to vaccinate and microchip the entire world populace?

Or the Corporatocracy's latest testing of how effective is its hold over the mass of people?

Take your pick. Personally, I cannot help but think that my ex-wife has something to do with it. (I just smirked, in case you were wondering).

Adolf Hitler not only designed the modern State but pioneered its methods of mass psychology. He wrote that since the people do not think, but feel, only a big lie will sway the masses. Or in the words of the corrupt Senator Roark in the film *Sin City,*

"Get the people to say yes to what they know in their hearts is bullshit and they'll be yours for life."

As I asked a woman on the bus recently,

"Is anybody you know sick with the virus?"

"No there isn't, all this panic is pretty strange, but I'm staying at home because I was told to and I don't want to lose my job."

Tyranny is never imposed on us by anyone but ourselves. Once we are mentally shackled, the police state follows because it can.

On the other hand – and please take note of this - tyranny begins to crumble when it is first denied in ourselves by our taking responsibility for it.

Unfortunately, Adolf was right: human beings are emotional, not rational. We are all trained by the raised hand of the parent or the state that to think and take responsibility for ourselves is disruptive, disobedient, and illegal. Go along and you will get along is society's gospel: even when "along" leads over a cliff.

What I have learned from the survivors of extreme torture and from my own inner changing is that genuine recovery happens when we can see our suffering in its bigger context. That is why I often show Indian residential school casualties the legal forms that their parents were forced to sign that incarcerated them, or the statutes that made the genocide legal. *"I see who's to blame now"* people will say, as a flicker of strength grows in their eyes.

So too must it be said of all of us in the present trauma. What we are enduring is the consequence of what we have sown. We too must see who and what is to blame, by looking deeply in the mirror held up by the ones who we have helped imprison and destroy.

For too many years I have tried to get my own people to do exactly that. I failed, of course. The charade continues unchecked. But that is never the issue. I could not have done anything else.

One of my Hastings street buddies is a Viet Nam veteran and a former college professor named Nathan. Like me, Nat got vomited out of his profession and dwells now on the margins of our madness. Recently I watched him as he undertook a devastating rant against a crop of well meaning and stupid church people who were bringing to the homeless folks the candy, pop, and other trash they think the poor need.

Nathan was his usual brilliant self that day. He took a deep breath and exclaimed at the astonished Christians,

"You're just the blind leading the blind! Just look around you! We've all made a pact with Satan to prosper at the expense of others and live off the blood-soaked fruits of empire! None of us have cared how many Indians and children and good people had to be sacrificed to keep us safe and happy. But now that Satan's presenting his bill to us for services rendered, we all want to wiggle out of the consequence of selling our souls! Forget it! There's no way out for any of us, we're too sick and corrupt. None of us can be saved from our own insanity. We've lost the right to survive!"

Take it or leave it.

The point for me is that, even as I tried exorcising the malignant spirit from my people, I forgot that Jesus himself discovered that some demons are too strong to be cast out of those they possess. And thus it is with the monstrous, planet-eating machine that we all depend on for survival. None of us can willingly step out from its enthralling and suicidal embrace. We must be thrown out. But even among those of us who have been so exiled, who will persist in the wilderness and seek a better home?

Is the exodus from our own Sodom possible even for a handful of just souls?

After all these years and battles, I find myself back again in the Lotus pub with dear old Joe Hendsbee, but with a difference: for now, I am the hardened veteran speaking of who I am to young seekers.

I have finally come to know Joe's assurance and wear some of his battle honors, along with the scars that prove that we still bear hearts that live and have earned our own liberty. And just as Joe Hendsbee and Don Eperson and so many like them have kept me moving through all the carnage of the years with my sword held aloft, so do unseen and flagging spirits light their own torch from my flame: especially in these final days.

Just before he was hanged by the Nazis in 1945, Dietrich Bonhoeffer wrote:

What we need is not geniuses, or clever tacticians, but plain and honest people who are willing to act whatever the risk and without counting the cost. Will our inward power of resistance be strong enough, our honesty with ourselves remorseless enough, for us to find our way back to ourselves?

The question remains, as Sodom recedes and nothing but the desert yawns before a few of us. But my heart drinks even more deeply now from this oasis of hope passed down to us beleaguered pilgrims by William Wordsworth:

Though nothing can bring back the hour of splendour in the grass, of glory in the flower, We will grieve not, rather find strength in what remains behind;
In the primal sympathy which having been must ever be;
In the soothing thoughts that spring out of human suffering;
In the faith that looks through death;
In years that bring the philosophic mind –
Thanks to the human heart by which we live,
Thanks to its tenderness, its joys, and fears.
To me the meanest flower that blows
Can give thoughts that do often lie too deep for tears.

About the Author

There is too much to tell, really, so we settled on this version:

Kevin Daniel Annett (one of his many pseudonyms) was conceived in a secret chamber of the Soviet Politburo in Moscow. The identity of his parents is unknown but there are several suspects.

Trained in the art of espionage and subversion at a young age, Comrade Kev was landed by a Russian submarine on the shores of Hudson's Bay from where he spread out across the prairies sowing seeds of discontent and rebellion. Assigned as a teenager to instigate an insurrection in Vancouver, Kev found the going there tough among the lotus-eating, latte-sipping crowd and he was forced to enter deep cover.

Over many years our Hero fomented revolution under the guises of a steelworker, an itinerant philosopher, a professional student, a whistle-blowing clergyman and a cheeky Nobel Peace Prize nominee. Eventually the mask slipped when his efforts toppled the Roman papacy and a Vatican hit team tried unsuccessfully to kill him with a banana.

At that point Kev's illegitimate son, Justin Trudeau, with instructions from his Jesuit handlers and psychiatrist, promptly blew the whistle on his Dad. His cover blown, Kevin went on Oprah and told all. The movie rights to his life story have been sold to the Weinstein Brothers.

Retired now from the Communist apparatus with the rank of a Red Army Colonel, Kev is enjoying his sixth age of lean and slippered pantaloon in the north end of Winnipeg in a luxury condo just above Zuken's Perogy and Blintz Emporium.

Kev spends his days composing his memoirs and instructing young followers in small arms training, the Common Law and Social Un-Distancing. He is the author of seventeen books. Kevin likes women who use big words, although he is willing to settle for anyone without serious substance abuse issues or too many warts.

To read other books and productions by Kevin, see www.murderbydecree.com , which also contains all the evidence cited by him in this book.

You can actually write to the sorry bastard c/o thecommonland@gmail.com or in a pinch just try angelfire101@protonmail.com . Otherwise, leave a note for Kev on the bulletin board of the Alley Katz Bowling Lanes in Biggar, Saskatchewan.

This book was published during the spring months of 2020 in the Republic of Kanata, formerly the painfully boring police state known as Canada.

Now get off your ass.

And you thought you knew about Canada ...

The Land of No-One
The play that Canadians do not want to see

Twice shut down during its attempted production in Canada, **The Land of No-One** is about the dark underbelly of the "nice" nation to the North.

The play's protagonist is a happy family man and a pillar of the community who also has the blood of the innocent on his hands. A former church missionary doctor who experimented on and killed aboriginal children, Dr. Oliver Pierpoint must face his own skeletons and his family when a survivor of the crime comes forward. But how do the government and church that sponsored him respond? And is justice possible or even imaginable when the criminals are still in power?

The playwright, Kevin Annett, is a former United Church of Canada minister who was fired, defrocked, and blacklisted after exposing genocide in his own country and church, and giving a platform for aboriginal survivors. For over twenty years he has led the movement to force the truth and reparations from the government and churches of Canada for their proven crimes against humanity. He is an award-winning documentary filmmaker, writer, and human rights consultant. He has been nominated for the Nobel Peace Prize on two occasions and in 2016 received the coveted Prague Peace Award.

"I'm in exile from my own people and have learned the hard lesson that a culture in denial of itself must have the truth brought to it from the outside. I hope to do that on the stages and in the streets of America and among people not afraid of their shadow."

A pdf copy of **The Land of No-One** can be obtained from the author. Contact Kevin Annett at thecommonland@gmail.com . His books and work are found at www.murderbydecree.com .

No Flu Bug justifies a Police State

One morning in March Canadians awoke to find that our democracy had vanished: no more Parliament, no courts of law, no civil liberties. All of it was snuffed out in an instant by one man: Justin ("Mini P.") Trudeau. His Dad Pierre tried the same bullshit with his brief War Measures Act. But today's Police State is here to stay if the Son of Turdo gets his way.

How does Mini P's banning of free speech and making it a crime to criticize the government help fend off a flu virus? Crime Minister Justin is not saying, any more than he's explaining why he took bribes and obstructed RCMP investigations into his role in the SNC Lavalin scandal. That's all conveniently forgotten now that he's got Canadians scared of their own shadows, and neighbours.

But here is what matters, people: everything Trudeau is doing is completely illegal. Neither a court order nor Parliament have authorized his suppression of our freedoms. He is acting alone as one guy, not an accountable official. Trudeau's orders are against the law, so they have no authority over us and can be ignored.

If you don't ignore Trudeau's fraudulent and treasonous orders you're colluding in a crime. That goes for every Mountie, cop, soldier and civil servant in Canada, too. The only legal and moral thing for ALL of us to do is to stand down Trudeau's one-man dictatorship by not cooperating with it. We must return to democracy and the rule of law.

As for the COVID flu scare, the infection and death rate from Corona is far below that of last year's flu outbreak. Most people who get sick from it have mild or medium reactions. "Social Distancing" does nothing to protect people from getting sick. You are being fed an enormous lie, people, to justify a plan by Trudeau's Big Pharma backers to inoculate everyone with microchips. Bill Gates even admits that.

Don't give in to their plan or to fear. Join our growing Resistance to the global corporate dictatorship. Start by doing three things**: Ignore Trudeau's orders. Refuse to Distance or Quarantine. And Refuse all Mandatory Vaccinations.**

But go further and take back Canada for all the people. Join the movement to establish a Republic where people govern themselves, so that this police state and corporate tyranny can never happen again. Act now while you still can. Live Free or Die!

Tune in every Sunday to the Voice of the Resistance and the Republic at 3 pm pacific and 6 pm eastern on www.bbsradio.com/herewestand . Contact us at republicofkanata@gmail.com and see www.murderbydecree.com .

Printed in Dunstable, United Kingdom